T0245650

THE COMPLETE PLANT-BASED COOKBOOK FOR BEGINNERS

2025

THE COMPLETE
PLANT-
BASED
COOKBOOK
FOR BEGINNERS

110+ WHOLE FOOD RECIPES FOR A HEALTHY LIFESTYLE

JL FIELDS

PHOTOGRAPHY BY TARA DONNE

callisto
publishing
an imprint of Sourcebooks

Copyright © 2020, 2024 by Callisto Publishing LLC
Cover and internal design © 2024 by Callisto Publishing LLC
Interior and Cover Designer: Lindsey Dekker
Art Producer: Hannah Dickerson
Editor: Rachel Feldman
Production Manager: Michael Kay
Production Editor: Melissa Edeburn
Photography © 2020 Tara Donne. Food styling by Cyd McDowell. Illustrations © Statement Goods/Creative Market, interior pattern; BlackBird Foundry/Creative Market, p. V. Author photo courtesy of Allison Moix.

Originally published as *The Complete Plant-Based Diet: A Guide and Cookbook to Enjoy Eating More Plants* in the United States of America by Callisto Publishing, an imprint of Callisto Publishing LLC.

Published by Callisto Publishing LLC C/O Sourcebooks LLC
P.O. Box 4410, Naperville, Illinois 60567-4410
(630) 961-3900
callistopublishing.com

Printed and bound in the United States of America

For Dad

CONTENTS

INTRODUCTION

For the early part of my adult life, it never occurred to me to eat a vegetarian diet. A devoted meat-and-potatoes gal from the Midwest, I was living healthfully and happily with my status quo.

In my late thirties, I found myself in a small village in Kenya for a pretty cool work assignment that concluded with a gorgeous celebration of song and dance and the slaughter of a goat, which was then served for dinner. As a child, growing up on the Mississippi River and straddling Illinois and Iowa, I knew all about meat and how it landed on our plates. But something felt different. I looked that goat in the eye, and I became a vegetarian that night. Over the course of eight years, I slowly inched toward fully plant-based eating and vegan living, which I've been doing for more than 10 years.

Some longtime followers of my vegan culinary work and cookbooks may be scratching your heads (and a few may be picking yourselves up from the floor). I've always been very clear that I identify as "vegan," not "plant-based." But let's be clear: "vegan" is a noun, and so am I. "Plant-based" is an adjective that describes a way of eating that just happens to be the way I tend to cook. Confused? Don't worry, I'll explain these distinctions soon enough. The trend toward plant-based eating continues to grow, and I want to make it easy and less confusing to adopt a plant-based diet.

If you picked up this book, you're probably not sure where to start. And I get that. As much as I'm a vegan culinary enthusiast now, I struggled when I first started eating plant-based. Where's my protein? Just what am I supposed to do with kale? Nutritional yeast, what is that? I also wondered: Do I have to shop at specialty grocery stores? Have I just signed up for the world's most expensive way of eating? Will I ever be able to dine out with friends again?

It didn't take long to discover that beans and legumes (and lots of veggies and grains) have protein, as well as plenty of vitamins and nutrients. I learned that beans, grains, vegetables, and fruit are absolutely affordable. And that anything plant-based I want to find is at my local grocery store, Walmart, Target, or even Costco.

When I started eating plant-based, I lived with a non-veg husband. I learned to create meals that he enjoyed as much as I did (spoiler alert: after a few years, he went vegan, too). I took cooking classes in New York and Philadelphia and learned the art and craft of making vegan cheese and meat and how to cook with the seasons.

What does that mean for you? This book is for *everyone*. Throw those labels aside. If you eat food, you eat vegetables. And I've got some tasty ones for you. If you recently watched a documentary about the health benefits of a plant-based diet or your physician suggested you eat more plants, I've got the goods right here. This is a plant-exclusive cookbook that will help you eat healthy food—layered with flavors for your pleasure palate—every day.

From an introduction to plant-based eating to pragmatic tips for making this way of eating sustainable to culinary tricks that will leave you feeling like a chef, plus a 21-day meal plan to help make things easy and 115 easy recipes that will appeal to you and to those you cook for, this book has everything you need.

I want you to fall in love with leafy greens, fragrant fruit, protein-packed legumes, nutrient-rich grains, and all the nuts and seeds that fall in between. I want you to have fun in the kitchen and to feel like a culinary rock star (with as little effort as possible).

And I think you will.

PART ONE

The Joy of Plant-Based Cooking

Okay, are you ready to get excited about plants? You should be. It's a whole new world. When I was a child growing up in rural Illinois, we had a big garden and grew lots of our own food. We even canned the tomatoes we harvested and froze corn to eat during the winter. But we never really focused on the beauty of the plant. It was always on the side of the plate, an afterthought to the meaty center. When I went vegan, it was like meeting these veggies for the first time. As you cook your way through this book, I want you to experience the pure joy of making bountiful produce shine.

Rethink your plate!

CHAPTER 1

THE PLANT-FORWARD PLATE

A plant-exclusive plate looks different from the Standard American Diet plate. It's fresh and vibrant: the center-piece is veggies, legumes (which can include tofu and tempeh), or seitan (a delicious approach to "wheat meat"), accompanied by hearty grains, creamy nut-based sauces, and juicy pieces of fruit. The plant-based plate is abundant, and so good for you.

In this chapter, you'll learn what foods are best to fill your plant plate. Along the way, you'll discover just how darn delicious a plant-based diet can really be. Not to mention how much fun it is—I mean, riced cauliflower, heart-of-palm scallops, and watermelon fries are tasty, and super cool to make.

For the Love of Plants

You've probably heard about the plant-based diet from a friend or read about it in the news. You may have noticed an increasing amount of plant-based foods at the grocery store and in restaurants. There are documentaries, books, and even music devoted to the lifestyle. It's true—the trend is hot, hot, hot!

Of course, vegetarian and plant-based diets are nothing new—they've been around for centuries. But the word "vegan" didn't become part of our vocabulary until the 1940s, when Donald Watson and friends at the United Kingdom's Vegan Society took the word VEGetariaAN and made "vegan" to broadly cover the choice to avoid the consumption and use of animals. In the early 1980s, the term "plant-based" surfaced as a result of health studies; more people began to choose a plant-forward diet for reasons not necessarily focused on the ethics of eating animals. This plant-based diet introduced a "whole-food, plant-based" approach, which also included restrictions on some vegan foods, such as sugar, salt, and vegetable oil.

Although health and animal rights have long been motivating factors for adopting vegan and plant-based diets, a newer factor has emerged over the past decade. As the climate continues to change, environment-focused individuals and groups are connecting the dots to animal agriculture, and as a result, plant-based eating has become a talking point and moral approach to protecting the earth.

There is no one age group or motivation driving this demand. I teach vegan cooking classes in Colorado Springs, and my students range in age from 16 to 80. Some want to reduce their carbon footprint, others want to get off their cholesterol medicine, and still others are trying to cook healthier to help a loved one reverse type 2 diabetes. You know what they all want? Good food.

And in this book, we're making good food that's good for you.

BENEFITS WORTH CELEBRATING

Healthy heart. Following a plant-based diet can significantly lower cholesterol levels. Why? There is no cholesterol in plants. Zip, zilch, nada. Why does that matter? Lower cholesterol levels can prevent heart attacks and heart disease.

Pro tip: If you're grocery shopping for vegan foods and you find the ingredients on a label confusing, look for the cholesterol—if you see "0," it's vegan.

Disease prevention and reversal. Now add a three-quarters to one-half lower rate of high blood pressure, a two-thirds lower risk if type 2 diabetes, and up to a 20 percent lower risk of cancer. This is why so many physicians—and some large health insurance companies—recommend plant-based diets for their patients.

Better mood. Plant-based diets are high in brain-friendly vitamins like folate and B_6, which boost your mood. No wonder people feel happier eating this way.

Weight, what? Let's be honest. Some people are motivated to eat plants to lose weight. And that *could* happen. Weight loss is never a guarantee, but on average, vegans do have a lower BMI and less body fat than meat-eaters and vegetarians.

Save money. Some people think eating vegan means spending lots of money, but that's not so, especially if you eat plant-based foods cooked at home. Buy dried beans and grains in bulk, opt for fresh produce over packaged foods, swing by big box stores like Costco and Sam's Club, and meal plan (I can help with that—see chapter 3), and you'll set yourself up for spending less.

Reduce your carbon footprint. Eat vegan, and you could reduce your carbon footprint by 73 percent. Yep, you read that right. Global meat and milk production are responsible for 60 percent of agricultural greenhouse gas emissions. And a plant-based diet also reduces land and water use.

What I Mean by "Plant-Based"

In a world full of labels, this plant-based thing can get really confusing. Ask five people who eat plant-based and you just might find five different descriptions of the diet. And they could all be right! But I'm not interested in right and wrong; I just want to be clear about my intention. Throughout this book, when I say we're eating plant-based, I mean we're eating plants, mostly whole, and definitely minimally processed. What makes up a plant-based diet, period?

Vegetables

Fruits

Legumes

Grains

Nuts and seeds

Let's dig into the food language a little more.

100 percent plants. I use no animal-derived foods or ingredients in this book. Yes, that includes honey.

Whole foods. I'm not relying on overly processed foods or ingredients in these recipes. Some lightly processed foods that I use, on occasion, include whole-grain bread and pasta, tofu, tempeh, unsweetened plant-based milk, and some vegetable and fruit oils.

Minimal salt, oil, and sugar. To clear up any confusion: vegetable oil is vegan, as is salt and some sugar. But I won't use much vegetable oil or sugar and will rarely use salt in any of the recipes (I will occasionally note them as "optional" or share a way to incorporate them in the recipe notes). As a chef and a foodie, I like a little salt or a sodium-forward ingredient here and there, but many people turning to a plant-based diet are trying to move away from a diet that relies heavily on salt and sugar. I want you to reacquaint yourself with your taste buds, which means learning how to use natural ingredients and new techniques to bring out flavors that enhance rather than mask the beauty of plant-based foods. You'll see a bit more vegetable oil and salt used in my homemade condiments and sauces (chapter 9), which are used sparingly in the recipes. You can always omit oil and salt to your preference.

PLANT-BASED, WFPB, VEGAN . . . OH MY!

Vegan: At its very root, vegan is an ethical decision. It's enacted by avoiding the consumption of, as well as the use of, animals and animal-derived products. This includes everything from food to clothing to health and household items to entertainment to avoiding the use of—and cruelty to—animals. Veganism is a lifestyle, rather than a diet. Therefore, someone who identifies as vegan may also eat a whole-food, plant-based diet, or they may eat vegetable oil and vegan sugar, and use some salt. Or, like me, they might do both, because one can be ethically motivated *and* health-conscious.

Plant-based: A plant-based diet is, technically, based on plants: fruits, vegetables, whole grains, legumes, and nuts and seeds. That word "based" has caused some confusion. For some it means no animal products and only minimally processed foods. Others view it as eating more plant foods as their base, but also including animal products (there are even meat companies now blending animal meat with veg-etables and calling these products "plant-based"). Still others use it to describe how they eat (no animals) but not their lifestyle (they may wear leather or use products tested on animals). "Plant-based diet" and "whole-food, plant-based diet" are often used synonymously.

Whole-food, plant-based (WFPB): Like the plant-based diet, this way of eating is also based on fruits, vegetables, whole grains, and legumes. However, some have taken it further by eliminating salt, oils, and refined sugar (often abbreviated as SOS), and even nuts. People who follow the whole-food, plant-based diet avoid processed products like prepackaged meals. WFPB is not synonymous with vegan.

Building a Balanced Meal

The number-one questions most people have when they consider a plant-based diet are about nutrition: *Where do I get my protein? What about calcium? Do I need to take supplements?*

All these questions are understandable, simply because most of us grew up eating meat, so we think we know what our plate is supposed to look like. To dive into plant-based eating means learning to re-create that plate. The recipes in this book will help you do so while also producing nutritionally balanced dishes. You'll also find nutritional information for each recipe to help you craft the balanced diet you need.

Powerful Proteins

Plants have protein, my friends, so you're going to get plenty of protein if you're eating a plant-based diet. But that isn't to say you don't need to put some thought into your protein sources. The general recommendation for healthy adults is at least 0.36 grams of protein per pound of body weight daily. You may require more or less based on age, level of physical activity, and other personal needs. Just how much, exactly? That's a great question for your health care provider.

There is a long-standing assumption that vegans need to "combine proteins" to get a "complete protein." That information is out of date. "Complete protein" refers to the nine essential amino acids we obtain from foods we eat that complement the amino acids our bodies produce. Plant-based foods with these essential amino acids include quinoa, buckwheat, hempseed, and whole sources of soy—tofu, tempeh, miso, and edamame. (Speaking of soy, yes, it's plant-based, and yes, it's incredibly nutritious. Avoid it if you're allergic, obviously.)

So what's the best way to get protein? Simply focus on eating sufficient calories daily and be sure to eat at least three servings of beans/legumes each day. Here's what that can look like:

PLANT-BASED PROTEIN	SERVING SIZE	PROTEIN
Tempeh	3 ounces	16.8 g
Hemp seeds	3 tablespoons	10 g
Edamame (shelled)	½ cup	9.2 g
Tofu	3 ounces	9 g

PLANT-BASED PROTEIN	SERVING SIZE	PROTEIN
Pea milk	8 ounces	8 g
Peanuts	1 ounce	7.3 g
Black beans (cooked)	½ cup	7 g
Chickpeas (cooked)	½ cup	6 g
Quinoa (cooked)	½ cup	4 g

Complex Carbs

Carbohydrates have gotten a bad rap in today's diet culture. But not all carbs are created equal: There are good, better, and best carbs to choose from. Complex carbs are found in starchy foods like whole grains, beans, peas, vegetables, and, yes, bread and pasta. Simple carbs occur naturally in fruit but also in refined sugars and processed items such as soft drinks, syrups, and candy. You should aim to get 45 to 65 percent of your daily calories from whole-food sources of carbohydrates. Here are some plant-based foods that are great sources of carbohydrates:

- Beets
- Sweet potatoes
- Pumpkin
- Quinoa
- Barley
- Oats
- Apples
- Bananas
- Blueberries
- Oranges
- Kidney beans
- Chickpeas

Filling Fats

We used to be told that any fat was bad; now we have some diets telling us to eat mostly fat. The bottom line is that a dose of healthy fats is important in a vegan diet. Mono- and polyunsaturated fats are heart-healthy fats and improve the ratio of LDL ("bad") to HDL ("good") cholesterol. Good sources of healthy fats include:

- Avocado
- Walnuts
- Peanuts
- Olives
- Pistachios
- Cacao nibs
- Chia, sunflower, pumpkin, flax, and hemp seeds

Vitamins and Supplements

A balanced plant-based diet will provide most of your vitamins and nutrients: calcium, iron, magnesium, phosphorus, potassium, zinc, selenium, folic acid, and riboflavin, as well as vitamins A, C, E, K, B_3, and B_6. Additionally, most vegans or plant-based eaters will need to take vitamin D and iodine supplements, and some vegans may need to supplement calcium and iron. All plant-based eaters should take a vitamin B_{12} supplement: 25 to 100 micrograms daily or 1,000 micrograms two to three times weekly. How to know which supplements you need? Talk to your health care provider!

NOW PUT IT ALL TOGETHER

So how do we break down this nutrition info for use in daily life? Here are some of my favorite combos for pulling together balanced meals:

- Plain soy yogurt + rolled oats + chia seeds
- Lentils + quinoa and leafy greens + avocado slices
- Black beans + steamed sweet potatoes + cacao nib mole sauce
- Tempeh + roasted Brussels sprouts + toasted pistachios
- Chickpea hummus + whole-grain tortilla + tahini sauce
- Air-fried tofu + toasted millet + peanut sauce

When you begin to plan your meals in this way, you're not only nourishing your body, you're also empowering yourself to make healthy choices that satisfy your palate.

Noteworthy Ingredients

By now it's pretty clear that our focus is on five food groups: vegetables, fruit, legumes (beans), grains, and nuts and seeds. But what are some of the ingredients we're going to use to transform those basics into delicious meals? Glad you asked.

Seasonings

Acidic fruit juices. Lemon, lime, orange, and grapefruit juices add flavor to cooked dried beans (yep, they can stand in for salt) and are terrific in massaged kale salads.

Dried herbs and spices. Where to start? Chili powder, ground cinnamon, ground cumin, garam masala, smoked paprika, hot curry powder, and more. Getting to know a variety of spices is going to change the flavor profile of so many simple meals.

Fresh herbs. Sometimes you want the leafy green version of your favorite dried seasoning. Fresh mint, basil, parsley, and cilantro add flavor *and* a splash of color.

Liquid aminos and coconut aminos. For a more wholesome approach to soy sauce or tamari, try liquid aminos. Like soy sauce and tamari, traditional liquid aminos are soy-based (non-GMO and organic), but they have less sodium and no chemical preservatives and are gluten-free. Coconut aminos are a soy-free version made from fermented coconut sap. Both versions can be found at many grocery stores and at most health food stores.

Mirepoix. Is this term unfamiliar? There's a good chance you're making mirepoix all the time by sautéing onion, celery, and carrot as the beginning step in many recipes, from soups and stews to simple beans and grains. On page 49, you'll learn how to make an oil-free version of this culinary classic.

Miso. This fermented soybean paste is a magical condiment packed with nutrients, including protein, zinc, copper, and vitamin K. It can be found in a variety of colors—white, yellow, and red—with flavors ranging from light to stronger. The rich sodium flavor makes it a great substitute for salt, so it's the consummate umami ingredient in my cooking. Find it near the water-packed tofu in most grocery stores. Use it in cold dishes to retain probiotics; use it in hot dishes because it's so darn good.

Nutritional yeast. This deactivated yeast is high in protein and B vitamins (if you choose a fortified version) and adds a cheesy, nutty flavor to anything you use it on, from salads to steamed veggies to popcorn. It also thickens bean-based gravy and veggie-based sauces.

Soy sauce and tamari. Another fermented soy product, these briny sauces offer a liquid approach to adding umami. Use them in sauces, in salad dressings, or simply as an alternative to salt when finishing off rice and bean dishes. Tamari is a bit thicker than soy sauce, has less sodium, and is often gluten-free (be sure to read the label if you are sensitive to gluten).

Vinegars. Balsamic, apple cider, white, and rice vinegars are a great way to add a punch of flavor to the simplest vegetable. Drizzle a little rice vinegar over asparagus before grilling or balsamic vinegar over sweet potatoes before roasting, and you create an entirely new flavor with little effort.

Seeds

Chia seeds. Chia seeds can be ground in a coffee grinder or mill and simply sprinkled over vegan yogurt and granola for breakfast or over steamed vegetables. Add them to a mixture of soy milk and oats, and they will plump up to thicken it to a pudding consistency.

Flaxseed. Ground flaxseeds make an egg-cellent replacement for eggs (see what I did there?). Just whisk together 1 tablespoon ground flaxseed and 3 tablespoons warm water until blended, then use the mixture in place of eggs in the batter for wholesome banana nut bread or pancakes.

KICKED-UP VINEGAR

For an inexpensive way to add variety to the vinegars you use in dressings and when cooking, you have to try this **Fruity Balsamic Vinegar.** Think a holiday kale salad massaged in cranberry vinegar or a summery romaine salad tossed in a pineapple vinegar. All you need is:

¼ cup chopped dried fruit

1 cup balsamic vinegar

In a pint jar, combine the fruit and vinegar and cover with an airtight lid. Let sit at room temperature overnight or up to 3 days. Strain the mixture into another jar and cover with an airtight lid. Reserve the fruit for another use (toss it with vegetables before roasting or purée it into the Cashew Cream, page 182). Store at room temperature for up to 7 days or refrigerate for up to 2 weeks.

Hemp seeds. These nutty, protein-rich seeds are great sprinkled over salads or grain dishes for a boost of texture.

Sesame seeds. These versatile seeds can be ground into a paste (known as tahini) or sprinkled whole over a simple stir-fry.

Thickeners

Arrowroot powder. This gluten-free starch is ground from a tuber and can be used to naturally thicken sauces and gravies (while also adding protein). It's great sprinkled on tofu or potatoes and it adds a bit of puffy crunch to air-fried foods.

Tapioca flour. Mostly known as a gluten-free flour, this cassava root powder adds the ooey-gooey stretch you're looking for in plant-based cheese.

Sweeteners

Dates. This sweet little dried fruit is a great addition to your plant-based pantry. Pit, chop, and add them to a simple bowl of muesli and unsweetened plant-based milk, and you've bumped up the sweet factor and added some vitamins, nutrients, and minerals to your breakfast. They are great at binding together ingredients to create super-healthy "truffles" and energy bars. Any date will do, but Medjool dates— admittedly more expensive than others—boast more nutrition and are a culinary delight to work with. You can find them with the dried fruit in most grocery stores.

Dried fruit. Though not as nutritionally comparable to dates, and definitely not better than fresh fruit, dried fruit without added sugar is a great way to satisfy that sweet tooth.

Pure maple syrup. Dark maple syrup is my go-to, everyday sweetener of choice. I'm not saying this is a health food—it still adds sugar—but at least you'll get some riboflavin, calcium, zinc, and potassium, too. It's available at nearly any grocery store, usually in the breakfast aisle near the pancake mixes.

Enjoying Real Flavors

I hope you're beginning to see how plant-based eating can be more than just good for you—it can be just plain *good*. And you have the power to make this happen. In my cooking classes I try to encourage my students to tap into their intuitive cooking self. Of course, I know you want recipes (that's why I'm writing this book), but it doesn't hurt to learn a bit about how these recipes work so you can begin to grab vegetables and grains and beans and turn them into something special with little effort on your own.

Salty

Believe it or not, we don't add salt to give dishes a salty flavor; rather, salt brings out sweetness and tones down bitterness (think of the taste of a turnip or Brussels sprout before and after you've added salt). And salty tastes can come from ingredients beyond salt. We're talking about sodium chloride, and you can find it in plant-based ingredients such as miso paste and fermented or briny vegetables, as well as fresh beets, celery, carrots, and spinach.

Sweet

Sweet taste is often revealed as your palate changes by eating a plant-based diet. With a standard diet full of added and processed sweeteners many of us couldn't recognize the sweet already in front of us in the form of vegetables, whether raw or cooked, like carrots, sweet potatoes, beets, and butternut squash. Even citrus juice, like lime, or balsamic vinegar can make a bitter food sweeter.

Bitter

This taste concept usually evokes thoughts of an unpleasant or sharp flavor, but bitter ingredients can actually create sweetness and umami. Coffee, unsweetened cocoa, olives, and citrus zest are bitter by nature but we still enjoy them. Foods like kale, arugula, Brussels sprouts, and even walnuts can be bitter alone, but the addition of a sweet or umami ingredient makes them delicious. Conversely, adding a bitter food like kale to roasted butternut squash brings out the sweetness.

Sour

Acidity is probably the first thing that comes to mind, right? Lemon, grapefruit, and limes, for sure—but also tamarind (a tree pulp paste common in Indian cooking) and grapes. Fermented and briny foods, as well as vinegar, boast a sour flavor as well. Create a sweet salad and serve it with a sour soy sauce–rich stir-fry to experience bursts of flavor.

Umami

Umami is a savory, meaty essence not necessarily derived from meat-based ingredients. (Fun fact: I love umami so much, I had it tattooed on my arm.) Umami, the fifth flavor, brings a savory quality that adds a mysterious "wow" to a dish. Ripe tomatoes, mushrooms (dried and fresh), fermented foods (such as tempeh, sauerkraut, miso paste, and soy sauce), wine, and nutritional yeast create umami. Cooking techniques that enhance and create umami include caramelizing, roasting, grilling, and braising. Mix a little miso paste and veggie broth, spread it over the top of a head of romaine lettuce, add a little garlic and black pepper, then *grill* the lettuce for just a minute: the miso and the grilling turn a simple leafy green into a rich, savory veggie.

PLANT-BASED EATING AROUND THE WORLD

One thing you may notice throughout this book is a nod to a variety of flavor profiles from plant-based cooking around the world. If you've dined out as a vegan or are eating plant-based already, you've probably discovered that some of the best options for your diet can be found at international eateries.

- Turkey and the Middle East give us falafel, pita, and hummus.
- Chinese meals center around wholesome tofu and vegetable dishes.
- From Japan you'll notice many macrobiotic-influenced recipes in this book, as well as vegan sushi.
- Greece teaches us how to balance acidic flavor in bean dishes and grape leaves stuffed with rice.
- Indian cuisine focuses on the aromatic additions of spices and herbs to simple bean and rice dishes, creating complex flavors.

CHAPTER 2

TOOLS FOR PLANT-BASED COOKING

Are you excited about creating gorgeous plant-based creations packed with flavor that are also good for you? I think most of us have the best intentions when it comes to eating healthfully, but sometimes time and life get in the way. Give yourself the gift of time as you go through this next chapter. Building up your pantry, sourcing ingredients, and planning are the keys to saving time and money but also in helping you prepare so you follow through on this commitment to eat happily and healthfully.

Shopping Secrets

Shopping plant-based *can be* complicated and expensive, but it doesn't have to be. Here are some tips for keeping things easy and budget-friendly without losing on quality.

You don't have to buy organic. But for some produce you may want to. The Environmental Working Group's "Dirty Dozen," an annual list that shows the conventionally grown vegetables and fruits with the highest levels of pesticides, includes strawberries, spinach, nectarines, apples, peaches, pears, cherries, grapes, celery, tomatoes, sweet bell peppers, and potatoes. If you can afford to buy organic versions of these foods, consider doing so. Joining a local CSA (community-supported agriculture program) is a great way to get seasonal organic produce.

Buy in bulk to keep costs down. Beans and grains and are big part of the vegan diet. Buy them dry and in bulk, and you will save money *and* a few trips to the store. Similarly, big box stores like Costco and Sam's Club sell fresh veggies and fruit, as well as beans, grains, and nuts and seeds in bulk at cheaper prices.

Frozen and canned versions are okay. There's no shame in buying and using frozen and canned fruits and vegetables (just avoid brands with added sugars and check the sodium levels). Having both on hand can help you stay on track—and both can be cheaper than fresh.

It doesn't always have to be homemade. Homemade broth is delicious and the best way to control added sodium, but I'm the first one to admit that life gets in the way. If you're buying your broth, opt for low-sodium varieties. Same rule applies for condiments and sauces. Pick sauces with five or fewer ingredients. Sir Kensington's, Annie's Naturals, and even Hunt's offer good options.

Stop mincing ginger and garlic. Mealtime is easier when you can head to your refrigerator for a jar of minced ginger or garlic, rather than peeling and grating them fresh. Look for jarred products packed in water rather than oil and without added sodium.

Build your umami arsenal (slowly). To begin to create a symphony of flavors, you'll want to build up your cupboard, pantry, and refrigerator with umami. The good news is that many umami-rich refrigerated foods are fermented and last a very long time. There's no need to rush out and buy all these ingredients. Make a list and slowly begin to pick up items here and there.

- **At your local grocer:** Pick up pickled vegetables (sauerkraut, beets, and onions); nutritional yeast; soy sauce, tamari (labeled "gluten-free," if necessary), or liquid aminos; and smoky seasonings like paprika, chipotle chile powder, and liquid smoke.

- **At your local international market:** You'll find interesting fresh and dried mushrooms; a variety of pickled foods and hot sauces; and sea vegetables like dulse flakes, nori sheets, and kombu.

Use ripeness to your advantage. Fresh and ripe produce always wins. It tastes better, and the riper the fruit, the more nutritious it is, specifically when it comes to antioxidants and some vitamins. How do you know it's ripe?

- **Apples:** The stem easily twists off.

- **Asparagus:** Look for tightly closed buds and tender stalks.

- **Bananas:** Buy them green or bright yellow. Eat them when they're covered in brown spots and smell sweet.

- **Broccoli:** Look for bright green heads with closed floret buds.

- **Citrus:** Any citrus fruit is ready when it has reached its full color. It's overripe when the color begins to change again (limes will have yellow spots, for example).

- **Grapes:** They should be plump and thick and feel full of juice.

- **Leafy greens:** Look for a consistent color and crisp leaves. If some are soft or limp, they are past their prime.

- **Onions:** The skins should be dry and the texture should be firm.

- **Peaches:** Look for a round, slightly soft peach that has a sweet aroma.

- **Tomatoes:** Bright in color, plump, and slightly soft means they're ready.

Storage 101

There is nothing more frustrating than purchasing a big basket of colorful fruits and vegetables only to lose them to spoilage. Here are some tips for storage.

Fresh Produce

Store at room temperature:

- Bananas
- Cucumbers
- Garlic
- Onions
- Oranges
- Potatoes
- Sweet potatoes
- Winter squash

Store at room temperature, then move to the refrigerator when ripe:

- Avocados
- Melons
- Pears

Store in the refrigerator:

- Apples
- Asparagus
- Blueberries
- Broccoli
- Brussels sprouts
- Cabbage
- Cauliflower
- Corn (whole ears)
- Dark leafy greens
- Lemons
- Lettuce
- Limes
- Strawberries
- Summer squash

A NOTE ON HERBS

Wash fresh herbs in cool water, then dry them. (I use a square box colander that sits over the sink.) Wrap the herbs in a paper towel and store them in the refrigerator. If you want to make them last beyond a couple of days, trim an inch off the stems, set them in a jar filled with water, and store in the refrigerator. The one exception is basil: trim the stems and store in a jar of water on the counter, cutting the leaves as you need them. Freeze herbs for up to a year: blanch them (submerge in boiling water for one minute and then transfer to ice water immediately; this will preserve their color), then allow to fully dry before wrapping them in a paper towel and placing them in a zip-top plastic bag.

Pantry and Fridge Essentials

Regardless of where you're storing your ingredients, I have two key words for you: airtight containers. Mason jars, containers with snap lids, and even silicone resealable bags work great.

In my pantry:

- Dried mushrooms

- Dried seaweed: dulse flakes, kombu, nori sheets

- Dry grains: brown, white, and sushi rice; couscous; barley; millet

- Dry legumes: pinto, black, and kidney beans; chickpeas; lentils; split peas; black-eyed peas

- Nuts and seeds: walnuts, pecans, hazelnuts, pistachios

- Olive, canola, and avocado oils

- Shelf-stable unsweetened plant milk

- Spices, oh, so many spices: just enough for a small jar, as spices are best used within a year (see "In my freezer," below)

- Vegetable broth: I like to make my own, but I recommend going low-sodium if using store-bought

- Vinegars: balsamic, rice, apple cider, white

In my refrigerator:

- Condiments: hot sauces, ketchup, mustard
- Fermented and pickled veggies
- Ground flaxseed
- Miso paste
- Tempeh
- Tofu

In my freezer:

- Bulk seeds: sesame, chia, flax
- Bulk spices
- Fruit
- Tofu and tempeh
- Vegetables

Equipment You'll Need

You're not going to need anything terribly fancy to cook and prepare the recipes in this book and you probably have most of this equipment already. But I do want to share the kitchen equipment that I find helpful for preparing my plant-based goodies.

Sharp chef's knife. Operative word: sharp. A razor-sharp blade will do a better job of slicing and dicing, which means you can work faster and safer in the kitchen. (Because we're gonna be chopping a lot of veggies, y'all.)

Food processor and/or blender. These are helpful to create plant-based cheeses, sauces, and dressings. Many food processors can do double duty as a blender. Wide blenders can stand in for a food processor. Ninja makes a blending system that includes a blender, food processor, and even spiralizing blades (for making zucchini noodles), all on one base. It's one of my own most-used appliances.

12-inch skillet. Ideally one that is oven-safe (I love cast-iron skillets). This size will work for sautéing and panfrying.

Large saucepan or stockpot. If you want just one, opt for a 6- or 8-quart stockpot.

Large baking sheet. A 13-by-18-inch rimmed baking sheet is ideal for a standard oven and average kitchen size. Be sure it has a 1-inch rim. If you have a smaller oven or use a large toaster oven for baking, opt for a 9-by-13-inch rimmed baking sheet.

5- to 7-quart covered casserole dish or Dutch oven _(optional)._ Again, I love the cast-iron option, but it's simply a preference.

BEANS AND GRAINS IN AN INSTANT (POT)

Pressure cooking is the difference between cooking grains and beans in hours or in minutes. These days folks are adding a "multicooker" to their kitchen arsenal. These appliances have a pressure cooker function as well as the ability to slow cook, sauté, steam rice, and even make yogurt. Instant Pot, Cuisinart, Mealthy, Ninja, and Zavor are common brands. I strongly encourage you to invest in one if you can.

Cooking Fundamentals

Throughout this book you will learn to make the recipes, of course, but I want you to also feel comfortable walking into the kitchen and pulling a meal together yourself. By learning how to prepare your veggies and make your beans and grains, you'll realize you've *got* this.

Chopping Things

Coarsely chop: When exact size is less important because of the cooking method (blending, pressure cooking, etc.), you just want uniform pieces; aim for about 1 inch.

Chop: This is the most common vegetable prep instruction in this book. Aim for roughly ½-inch cubes.

Dice: Think of this as a smaller chop: about ¼-inch cubes.

Finely diced: These are smaller pieces, often used for garnish when you want a mini-burst of flavor.

Minced: Mostly used for garlic, minced pieces are very small, barely 1/8 inch. (If you buy jarred minced garlic, you won't have to bother with this step.)

Grated (shredded): If your box grater has multiple hole sizes, it can take care of grating vegetables, shredding vegan cheese, and even mincing ginger and zesting citrus if it has a "fine shred" or "zest" blade. (If not, you may want to invest in a Microplane grater, too.)

Spiralized: For "zoodles" (zucchini noodles) and other veggie noodles, use a spiralizer. Simply place the vegetable in the device (cut one end flat to face the blade first) and turn the crank or twist the vegetable, depending on your spiralizer. You can also use a knife or vegetable peeler to slice vegetables into ribbons.

Pressing Tofu

Most recipes using tofu will call for pressing and draining the tofu before using it. Here's how you do it:

1. Open the tofu package and drain the water.

2. Place a clean, lint-free dish towel or paper towels on a baking sheet.

3. Put the block of tofu on top of the towel(s) and wrap to cover the tofu.

4. Place a heavy pot on top of the wrapped tofu block.

5. Allow the tofu to drain for 10 to 20 minutes.

You can also invest in a tofu press and let it do the work for you. Some common brands include TofuXpress, EZ Tofu Press, and Tofuture.

Dry or Water Sautéing

The trick to sautéing without oil is to add just enough water or vegetable broth (which I prefer because umami) to cover the bottom of the pan. Bring the liquid to a boil over medium-high or high heat, then add the ingredients to be sautéed. Cover tightly and cook for about 2 minutes, then follow the rest of the recipe.

Cooking Beans

Canned beans are just fine for our plant-based cooking. But cooking dried beans from scratch saves money, *ensures* there's no added sodium or preservatives in your dish, and creates less waste than using canned beans. Here are the basics:

1. Put 1 cup dried beans in a heavy pot or saucepan, cover with 3 cups water, and set aside to soak overnight (up to 8 hours).

2. Drain and rinse the beans well.

3. Return the beans to the pot or saucepan. Cover with fresh cold water.

4. Bring the water to a boil over high heat, then lower the heat and simmer until the beans are tender, 1 to 1½ hours. (The exact cooking time will vary depending on the type and age of the dried beans. And if you live more than 3,000 feet above sea level, they will take even longer.)

Cooking Grains

Like beans, grains are a big part of the plant-based diet. The heartier and healthier the grain, the longer it will take to cook. The water needed to cook 1 cup dried grain can range anywhere from 1 cup to 2½ cups.

1. In a heavy saucepan with a tight-fitting lid, bring the water (see table on next page) to a boil over medium-high heat.

2. Rinse the grains, add them to the boiling water, and return to a boil.

3. Lower the heat, cover, and simmer until the liquid has been absorbed (you may need to add more water while the grain is cooking) and the grain is tender, 20 minutes to 1 hour, depending on the grain.

4. Remove from the heat, fluff the grain with a fork, replace the cover, and let sit for about 15 minutes before serving or using as directed in the recipe.

1 CUP GRAIN	LIQUID
Quinoa	2 cups
Brown rice	2½ cups
Farro	2½ cups
Millet	2½ cups
Cornmeal	4 cups
Steel-cut oats	4 cups

Plant-Based Milks and Sauces

Yes you *can* have creamy sauces and milks on a plant-based diet. How is this possible? Nuts and seeds! Cashews, almonds, walnuts, hemp seeds, flaxseed, and more can serve as the base for thick and rich sauces and simple homemade plant-based milk. You'll find recipes using sauces throughout the book and in chapter 9 (see page 177). But how to wing it, you ask? Usually I start by softening the nuts by soaking in water or bringing them to a boil with water. If you have a high-speed blender (such as Vitamix or Blendtec), you can often skip this step. For unsweetened plant-based milk, simply blend or purée nuts or seeds with water. For plant-based sauces, combine softened nuts with steamed or roasted vegetables, water, and tasty seasonings.

Here's a handy unsweetened plant-based milk formula:

1. Put 1 cup oats, almonds, or cashews in a bowl, add cold water to cover, and soak for 1 hour. Drain and rinse.

2. In a blender, combine the soaked oats or nuts and 4 cups fresh cold water. Blend on high for 1 minute.

3. Pour the puréed oats or nuts through cheesecloth or a nut-milk bag into the same bowl you used for soaking; discard the solids. Optionally (but highly recommended), strain the plant milk again through a fine-mesh strainer into a pitcher with a lid or another airtight container.

4. Cover and store in the refrigerator for up to 5 days.

Make It Easier: Make It Ahead

You may or may not know that I wrote the book *Vegan Meal Prep,* but what's important is that you know why I wrote it: it's how I cook. I'm a firm believer in making food over the weekend or on a day off specifically to have meals ready when I'm just too busy to cook. I've included a meal plan for you to try (see chapter 3), but here are some other simple steps you can take to make life easier.

Meal Plan

Save money by working with what you've got. Instead of going on autopilot at the grocery store, scan your pantry and refrigerator. With some dried or canned beans on hand, plus a grain or two, you can easily get ready for the week by mixing and matching them with produce that you already have or can pick up.

Tip: Plan meals on the basis of the items you decide to bulk cook (more on that below).

Meal Prep

Get ready for the week with a traditional meal prep: prepare overnight oats for breakfast and mason jar salads for lunch, and make two recipes that can be stored in containers ready to reheat for a fast dinner.

Batch Cook

Choose items that can be reused for other recipes. Beans and grains, roasted vegetables, and sauces are good places to start. For example, one big batch of black beans and Cheesy Chickpea Sauce (page 194) can set you up for a black bean hippie bowl, a black bean soup, or some delicious nachos. Cook some beans and grains, roast up vegetables, prepare salads, and whip up Cheesy Chickpea Sauce (page 194) and Tofu Sour Cream (page 181), and you'll have food and flavor at your fingertips.

A Plant-Based Dinner Party

I hope you're excited to start creating stunning meals. The next chapter offers a 21-day meal plan with weekly shopping lists and prep tips to help folks who are newer to plant-based eating get started. But if you're less into meal plans and more into free-styling, I've also provided this fun little dinner party menu. Or, why not use this menu to kick off your meal plan either way? Get your family and friends on board! Show them just how satisfying plant-based eating can be by throwing a plant party. Let's get all fancy with some wine pairings, too.

To Start
Avocado Sushi Rolls and Cream of Miso Mushroom Stew
Sancerre

The Main Event
Scalloped Hearts of Palm Provençal with Roasted Asparagus
Rosé or Gruet Brut

Sweet Ending
Chocolatey Mousse
Red Zinfandel

CHAPTER 3

21 DAYS OF PLANT-BASED EATING

If you're new to plant-based eating, it can be hard to know where to start. And even if you're not new, sometimes you're busy and just need someone to tell you what to eat. For all of the above, here's a basic 21-day plan that will show you how to get your five vegan food groups easily and flavorfully. You'll find all the recipes in this plan in part 2.

Using the Plan

This meal plan uses leftovers to make your life easier—because most of us don't have time to cook three meals a day. I'm also giving you some tips for what to prep each week. One thing you should know about meal planning and prepping: there is repetition. Trust me, you do *not* want to make 21 different meals each week. If you're worried about the amount of work or repetition, consider starting by making one less meal per week and opting for some yummy plant-based takeout instead (Mediterranean, Mexican, or Ethiopian, anyone?).

Adjusting Servings

This plan is designed for one person, but it's pretty easy to adjust to feed two or even four. Most of the recipes in this book yield two or four servings, which are easy to double. When you see a recipe that serves two, and you happen to be meal planning for two, double it. If you're feeding four, quadruple it. Meal prepping for one and see a recipe for four? Make the batch as is and freeze the leftovers (I'll let you know what freezes well and how to store extras).

Making Substitutions

I've organized the shopping lists into categories so you can easily see the types of foods you'll need. If you don't like certain foods or don't have particular items on hand, feel free to swap them out for a similar food. I include swapping tips for many recipes, but don't be afraid to experiment. Many of the recipes in this book rely on grains, beans, and leafy greens and vegetables, all of which lend themselves to substitutions.

A Note About Snacks

We're just focusing on the three square meals in this plan but, by all means, have a snack in the mid-morning, late afternoon, or evening. (Same goes for desserts, which you also find in chapter 8.) Here are my top 10 favorite plant-based snacks:

1. Baby carrots and snap peas (during Week 2, double up the hummus recipe and use it as a snack, too)

2. Apples or banana with nut butter

3. Cinnamon-and-Spice Granola (page 166), or store-bought granola

4. Nutty Date Truffles (page 170)—perfect for daytime snacking or dessert

5. Edamame

6. Super-Seed Chocolate Bark (page 175)

7. Endurance Bars (page 164), or store-bought plant-based protein bars

8. Cheesy Kale Chips (page 156)

9. Pistachios, almonds, or roasted soy nuts

10. Whole-grain crackers with salsa or Super-Green Guacamole (page 159)

Your Spice Arsenal

I've separated dried spices into a table (see below) so you can get a bird's-eye view of everything you'll need to have on hand from week to week.

Your Spice Arsenal

	WEEK 1	WEEK 2	WEEK 3
Anise seed		X	
Basil, dried			X
Black pepper	X	X	
Cayenne pepper		X	
Celery seed	X		
Chili powder		X	X
Chipotle chile powder		X	
Cinnamon, ground		X	X
Cumin, ground			X
Cumin seed	X		
Curry powder	X		
Fennel seed	X	X	X

	WEEK 1	WEEK 2	WEEK 3
Garlic powder	X		
Mustard, ground	X		
Mustard seed	X		
Nutritional yeast	X	X	X
Oregano, dried		X	X
Parsley, dried	X		
Red pepper flakes	X	X	X
Sage, dried			X
Salt, kosher	X		
Smoked paprika	X	X	X
Thyme, dried	X	X	X
Turmeric, ground	X		X

Week 1

	BREAKFAST	LUNCH	DINNER
MONDAY	Go-To Grits (page 61)	Massaged Kale Salad (page 82)	Cauliflower Florets 'n' "Cheese" (page 136)
TUESDAY	The Fruit Smoothie Formula (page 44)	Massaged Kale Salad (page 82)	Cauliflower Florets 'n' "Cheese" (page 136)
WEDNESDAY	Go-To Grits (page 61)	Veggie Lunch Muffins (page 91)	Loaded Green Curry (page 137)
THURSDAY	The Fruit Smoothie Formula (page 44)	Veggie Lunch Muffins (page 91)	Loaded Green Curry (page 137)
FRIDAY	Go-To Grits (page 61)	Loaded Green Curry (page 137)	Quinoa Pilaf (page 138)
SATURDAY	The Fruit Smoothie Formula (page 44)	Veggie Lunch Muffins (page 91)	Loaded Green Curry (page 137)
SUNDAY	Go-to Grits (page 61)	Veggie Lunch Muffins (page 91)	Quinoa Pilaf (page 138)

Buy This

OILS, VINEGARS, AND BROTHS
- Rice vinegar
- Vegetable broth, low-sodium (if you're not making your own)
- Vegetable oil spray

FRESH PRODUCE
- Broccoli (1 head)
- Carrot, large (1)
- Cauliflower (1 head)
- Fruit of your choice, fresh or frozen (2 cups, for smoothie)
- Garlic (6 cloves)
- Ginger (1-inch piece)
- Green onions (1 bunch)
- Green peas, fresh, frozen, or canned (10 ounces)

- Kale (2 bunches)
- Lemons, large (4)
- Parsley (or thyme) (¼ cup)
- Red bell pepper (1)
- Red onion, small (1)
- Spinach (16 ounces)
- Sweet potato, small (1)
- Tomato, large (1)
- Zucchini (1)

NUTS AND SEEDS
- Ground flaxseed
- Hemp seeds
- Peanuts
- Tahini
- Walnuts

BEANS/LEGUMES AND GRAINS
- Cannellini beans (one 15-ounce can)
- Chickpeas (one 15-ounce can)
- Cornmeal
- Quinoa

OTHER PACKAGED GOODS
- Coconut milk (one 16-ounce can)
- Miso paste
- Mushrooms, dried
- Unsweetened plant-based milk

Prep This

- One batch Spicy Umami Blend (page 196), which you'll use every week
- Go-To Grits (page 61)
- Kale and dressing for Massaged Kale Salad (page 82), cutting the recipe in half if you're only feeding one (store the kale and dressing separately until you're ready to eat)
- Cheesy Chickpea Sauce (page 194) for the Cauliflower Florets 'n' "Cheese" (page 136)

OPTIONAL PREP:
- Veggie Lunch Muffins (page 91; prep the night before eating)
- Individual-serving smoothie bags to use throughout the week
- Homemade Vegetable Broth (page 180) for the Quinoa Pilaf (page 138)—save leftover broth for Weeks 2 and 3

Week 2

	BREAKFAST	LUNCH	DINNER
MONDAY	Maple Muesli (page 54)	Spring Rolls with Pistachio Sauce (page 89)	Refried Jackfruit Tostadas (page 144)
TUESDAY	Maple Muesli (page 54)	Spring Rolls with Pistachio Sauce (page 89)	Refried Jackfruit Tostadas (page 144)
WEDNESDAY	Tempeh "Sausage" Patties (page 50)	Spicy Hummus Wrap(page 83)	Black-Eyed Pea and Sweet Potato Casserole (page 124)
THURSDAY	Maple Muesli (page 54)	Spring Rolls with Pistachio Sauce (page 89)	Black Bean Cauliflower Steak (page 127)
FRIDAY	Tempeh "Sausage" Patties (page 50)	Spicy Hummus Wrap (page 83)	Black-Eyed Pea and Sweet Potato Casserole (page 124)
SATURDAY	Fruity Yogurt Parfait (page 55)	Spring Rolls with Pistachio Sauce (page 89)	Black Bean Cauliflower Steak (page 127)
SUNDAY	Fruity Yogurt Parfait (page 55)	Spicy Hummus Wrap (page 83)	Black-Eyed Pea and Sweet Potato Casserole (page 124)

Buy This

OILS, VINEGARS, AND BROTHS

- Balsamic vinegar
- Rice vinegar
- Soy sauce or tamari, low-sodium
- Vegetable broth, low-sodium (if you're not making your own)
- Vegetable oil spray

FRESH PRODUCE

- Basil (4 ounces)
- Berries, any kind (2 cups)
- Carrot, large (1)
- Collard greens, fresh (16 ounces)
- Cucumber, large (1)
- Dates
- Garlic (6 cloves)
- Lemon, large (1)
- Onion, yellow (1)
- Serrano pepper (1)
- Sweet potatoes (1 pound)
- Swiss or rainbow chard (1 bunch)

NUTS AND SEEDS

- Almond butter
- Pecans
- Pistachios
- Sesame seeds
- Walnuts

BEANS/LEGUMES AND GRAINS

- Chickpeas (one 15-ounce can)
- Millet
- Refried beans, vegetarian (one 15-ounce can)
- Rolled oats
- Tortillas, corn (4)
- Tortillas, whole-grain (4)

OTHER PACKAGED GOODS

- Jackfruit (one 14-ounce can)
- Pure maple syrup
- Salsa, fresh or jarred (½ cup)
- Sun-dried tomatoes
- Spring roll rice papers (8)
- Unsweetened plant-based milk
- Tempeh (one 8-ounce package)
- Yogurt, plain vegan (2 cups)

Prep This

- Maple Muesli (page 54; double if you want to use it in the Fruity Yogurt Parfait)
- Veggies for the Spring Rolls with Pistachio Sauce (page 89), but hold off on wrapping the spring rolls until just before serving
- Hummus for the Spicy Hummus Wrap (page 83), but hold off on rolling the wraps until just before serving (save the aquafaba from the can of chickpeas to use for the tostadas)

OPTIONAL PREP:

- Beans and jackfruit for the Refried Jackfruit Tostadas (page 144)
- Tempeh "Sausage" Patties (page 50; prep the night before eating)
- Cashew Cream (page 182) for the Fruity Yogurt Parfait (page 55)

Week 3

	BREAKFAST	LUNCH	DINNER
MONDAY	Oatmeal-Raisin Breakfast Bowl (page 63)	Chick(pea) Pecan Salad (page 79)	Moroccan Eggplant Stew (page 104)
TUESDAY	Oatmeal-Raisin Breakfast Bowl (page 63)	Chick(pea) Pecan Salad (page 79)	Zoodle Spaghetti Marinara (page 131)
WEDNESDAY	Turmeric Tofu Scramble (page 49)	Yellow Dal Collard Wrap (page 85)	Moroccan Eggplant Stew (page 104)
THURSDAY	Oatmeal-Raisin Breakfast Bowl (page 63)	Chick(pea) Pecan Salad (page 79)	Turmeric Tempeh Stir-Fry (page 149)
FRIDAY	Turmeric Tofu Scramble (page 49)	Yellow Dal Collard Wrap (page 85)	Zoodle Spaghetti Marinara (page 131)
SATURDAY	Apple Avocado Toast (page 56)	Chick(pea) Pecan Salad (page 79)	Moroccan Eggplant Stew (page 104)
SUNDAY	Apple Avocado Toast (page 56)	Yellow Dal Collard Wrap (page 85)	Turmeric Tempeh Stir-Fry (page 149)

Buy This

OILS, VINEGARS, AND BROTHS

- Low-sodium soy sauce or tamari
- Vegetable broth, low-sodium (if you're not making your own)

- Apple, small (1)
- Avocado, large (1)
- Bell pepper, red (3)
- Bell pepper, yellow (1)
- Carrots, large (4)
- Celery (1 bunch)
- Collard greens (1 bunch)
- Cranberries, dried (¼ cup)
- Dates

- Eggplant, medium (1)
- Garlic (6 cloves)
- Kale (2 bunches)
- Leek (1)
- Lemon, large (1)
- Mushrooms, fresh, any kind (6 ounces)
- Onion, yellow (1)
- Zucchini (4), spiralized

NUTS AND SEEDS

- Pecans

BEANS/LEGUMES AND GRAINS

- Bread, whole-grain (4 pieces)
- Chickpeas (two 15-ounce cans)

- Steel-cut oats
- Yellow split peas, dried (1 cup)

OTHER PACKAGED GOODS

- Hearts of palm (one 14-ounce can or jar)
- Unsweetened plant-based milk

- Tofu (one 14-ounce package)
- Sun-dried tomatoes

Prep This

- Oatmeal-Raisin Breakfast Bowls (page 63; these store great in glass mason jars to tote to work and reheat)
- Chick(pea) Pecan Salad (page 79)
- Dal for the Yellow Dal Collard Wraps (page 85), but hold off on assembling the wraps until right before serving

OPTIONAL PREP:

- Guac for the Apple Avocado Toast (page 56; prep the night before eating)
- Turmeric Tofu Scramble (page 49; prep the night before eating)

PART TWO

The Best Plant-Based Recipes

Okay, let's get this cooking party started. We've covered the fundamentals, so it's time to put theory into practice. In other words: Time to make and eat all the food. In the recipes that follow, you'll find labels that will help you navigate dietary restrictions, determine how long a recipe will take, or pick no-fuss or no-cook recipes. These labels include:

- **5-ingredient:** These dishes require only five ingredients.
- **No-cook:** These dishes don't require any cooking.
- **One-pot:** You need only one vessel (such as one pot, one skillet, one pan, one baking dish) to cook these dishes.
- **Quick:** These dishes can be made in 30 minutes or less.

CHAPTER 4

BREAKFASTS AND SMOOTHIES

THE FRUIT SMOOTHIE FORMULA

PREP TIME: 5 minutes | **SERVES:** 2 | Gluten-free, Nut-free, Soy-free | 5-ingredient, No-cook, Quick

A firm proponent of clichés, I think every plant-based cookbook should begin with a smoothie recipe. But honestly, if you understand the basic formula for a quick breakfast drink, you'll always have a go-to healthy option. Combos I love: strawberries and blueberries, peaches and plums. If you opt for frozen fruit, you won't need the ice.

2 cups unsweetened plant
milk (see Tip)

2 cups chopped fresh or
frozen fruit

2 tablespoons ground
flaxseed

1 cup ice (optional, if using
fresh fruit)

Combine all the ingredients in a blender and purée for 30 seconds to 1 minute, until smooth and creamy.

ALLERGEN TIP: You can make this gluten-, nut-, or soy-free depending on the plant-based milk you use. If you want it to be free of all three, use pea milk or a seed-based milk.

PER SERVING (2 CUPS): Calories: 253; Saturated Fat: 1g; Total Fat: 8g; Protein: 10g; Total Carbs: 39g; Fiber: 7g; Sodium: 128mg

GORGEOUS GREEN SMOOTHIE

PREP TIME: 5 minutes | **SERVES:** 2 | Gluten-free, Soy-free | 5-ingredient, No-cook, Quick

A green smoothie is a great way to make sure veg-averse family members get their greens. If you have kids who are picky eaters, enlist their help when you make this one. Kale, spinach, and watercress are packed with vitamins, minerals, and fiber and are excellent in a fruity breakfast (or snack) drink.

¼ cup nut or seed butter
2 frozen bananas, peeled
4 cups tightly packed
  shredded leafy greens
2 tablespoons chia seeds

Combine all the ingredients in a blender and add 3 cups water. Purée for 30 seconds to 1 minute, until most of the green flecks have disappeared and the texture is smooth and creamy. If the smoothie is too thick, add more water, a little at a time, until desired consistency is reached.

INGREDIENT TIP: You know when you've had bananas on the counter for too long and you think, "Uh-oh"? Don't throw out those overripe bananas. Peel them and place them (whole) in a large airtight container or zip-top plastic bag and store them in the freezer for up to 3 months. They are great in smoothies and in desserts like Cherry Nice Cream (page 167).

PER SERVING (2 CUPS): Calories: 380; Saturated Fat: 2g; Total Fat: 22g; Protein: 12g; Total Carbs: 41g; Fiber: 13g; Sodium: 53mg

THE BERRY-BLEND BOWL

PREP TIME: 5 minutes | **SERVES:** 2 | Gluten-free, Soy-free option | No-cook, Quick

Açaí bowls are ubiquitous at health food stores and on breakfast menus at vegan restaurants. Typically, frozen açaí purée is served with granola, banana, and other fresh fruits. This recipe takes a more budget-friendly approach, relying on frozen blueberries and cherries for their rich colors and antioxidants. If you'd like to top with some fresh fruits, though, be my guest! I prefer soy milk for this bowl for its added protein and creaminess, but any plant-based milk will do.

2 cups unsweetened
  soy milk

1 cup frozen blueberries

1 cup frozen pitted cherries

2 bananas, sliced

1 cup Maple Muesli (page
  54) or granola

4 tablespoons hemp seeds

1. In a blender, combine the soy milk, blueberries, and cherries and purée until smooth. Divide the purée between two serving bowls.

2. Arrange the banana slices halfway around the edge of each bowl. Spoon ½ cup of Maple Muesli into the center of each bowl.

3. Spoon 2 tablespoons of hemp seeds around the edge of each bowl, opposite the bananas, and serve.

APPLIANCE TIP: Try using a food processor instead of a blender to make the berry purée. Since the purée is nice and thick, it can be much easier to get it all out of a food processor and into the serving bowls.

PER SERVING (2 CUPS): Calories: 540; Saturated Fat: 2g; Total Fat: 18g; Protein: 17g; Total Carbs: 84g; Fiber: 11g; Sodium: 129mg

BREAKFAST BUDDHA BOWL

PREP TIME: 10 minutes | **COOK TIME:** 35 minutes | **SERVES:** 4 | Gluten-free option, Nut-free | One-pot

I studied macrobiotic cooking in an intensive program with Christina Pirello the year I went vegan, and I was delighted to discover the joy of less conventional breakfast meals. From miso soup to braised root vegetables to hearty porridge, macro-focused breakfasts are packed with nutritious ingredients. This dish leans toward porridge, but to create a vegan classic, the addition of beans and leafy greens turns it into a stick-to-your-ribs way to start the day.

3 tablespoons rice vinegar

½ cup diced yellow onion

2 carrots, diced

1 cup amaranth

1 cup rolled oats

4 cups tightly packed leafy greens (kale, spinach, or Swiss chard)

1 (15-ounce) can adzuki beans, drained and rinsed

¼ cup nutritional yeast

2 tablespoons low-sodium soy sauce or tamari

1. In a large saucepan, heat the vinegar over medium-high heat until bubbling. Add the onion and carrots and cook until the onion is translucent, about 5 minutes.

2. Add the amaranth and 2½ cups water and bring to a boil.

3. Lower the heat to low and simmer for 10 minutes.

4. Add the oats, raise the heat to medium-high, and return to a gentle boil.

5. Add the leafy greens and adzuki beans and stir. Lower the heat to low and simmer until the mixture is thick and the oats are tender, 10 to 15 minutes more.

6. Remove from the heat and stir in the nutritional yeast and soy sauce, then serve.

SWAP IT: Adzuki beans are firm and nutty, and offer a hint of sweetness. If you can't find them, try kidney, red, or cranberry beans.

ALLERGEN TIP: To make it gluten-free, make sure to buy oats and tamari that are labeled "gluten-free."

PER SERVING (1½ CUPS): Calories: 414; Saturated Fat: 1g; Total Fat: 5g; Protein: 20g; Total Carbs: 73g; Fiber: 13g; Sodium: 364mg

TURMERIC TOFU SCRAMBLE

PREP TIME: 10 minutes | **COOK TIME:** 15 minutes | **SERVES:** 4 | Gluten-free, Nut-free | One-pot, Quick

You can change up the flavor profile of this flexible, nutrient-dense recipe with different spices and toss in whatever veggies you like. One thing I never change? Starting with mirepoix! The flavor base for so many delicious meals, mirepoix is 2 parts onion to 1 part carrot and 1 part celery. In my cooking classes I always say, "If you don't know what to have for dinner, start a mirepoix in the skillet and let the aroma inspire you from there."

2 tablespoons Vegetable
   Broth (page 180) or water
1 cup diced yellow onion
½ cup diced carrot
½ cup diced celery
1 (14-ounce) block
   extra-firm tofu, pressed
   (see page 23) and drained
1 teaspoon ground turmeric
½ teaspoon smoked paprika
½ teaspoon chili powder
2 cups tightly packed
   chopped kale
½ teaspoon salt or Spicy
   Umami Blend (page 196)

1. In a large skillet, heat the broth over medium-high heat. Add the onion, carrot, and celery and sauté until the onion begins to soften, about 3 minutes.

2. Crumble the tofu with your hands into the skillet. Add the turmeric, smoked paprika, and chili powder, stir well, and cook for 5 minutes.

3. Add the kale and stir well. Cover the skillet, lower the heat to medium-low, and cook for 5 minutes more.

4. Stir in the salt and serve.

MAKE AHEAD: Mirepoix is a great cooking staple to prepare in bulk over the weekend. Just sauté a bunch of onion, carrot, and celery (a ratio of 2:1:1) and store the mixture in an airtight container in the refrigerator to use as needed during the week.

PER SERVING (1 CUP): Calories: 123; Saturated Fat: 1g; Total Fat: 6g; Protein: 11g; Total Carbs: 9g; Fiber: 2g; Sodium: 44mg

TEMPEH "SAUSAGE" PATTIES

PREP TIME: 10 minutes | **COOK TIME:** 20 minutes | **MAKES:** 4 patties | Nut-free | Quick

When I tried tempeh for the first time, I wasn't a fan; I found it slightly bitter and dense. But I realized it just needed a little extra love, so I steamed it and it became tender and absorbed more flavors when cooked or marinated. You'll note the recipe calls for vegetable oil spray or aquafaba. Both are optional, but either one will add a little something special to the texture of the "sausage." Serve over sautéed greens and top with Caramelized Onion Jam (page 195).

8 ounces tempeh
2 tablespoons
  nutritional yeast
2 garlic cloves, minced
½ teaspoon smoked paprika
½ teaspoon fennel seed
¼ teaspoon anise seed
¼ teaspoon red
  pepper flakes
¼ teaspoon salt or Spicy
  Umami Blend (page 196)
¼ teaspoon freshly ground
  black or white pepper
Vegetable oil spray or
  3 tablespoons aquafaba
  (optional)

1. Preheat the oven to 400°F. Line a baking sheet with parchment paper or a silicone baking mat.

2. Place a steamer basket or trivet in a large saucepan. Pour in 2 cups water and bring to a boil over high heat. Place the tempeh in the steamer basket or on the trivet, cover, lower the heat to medium, and steam for 5 minutes.

3. Using tongs, transfer the tempeh to a food processor and break it into four large pieces. Pulse for a few seconds to break up the tempeh into large chunks. Add the nutritional yeast, garlic, paprika, fennel, anise, red pepper flakes, salt, and pepper. Pulse in short bursts, adding 1 or 2 tablespoons water as needed, until completely combined, with a chunky, dough-like texture.

4. Form the mixture into 4 patties about ½ inch thick and place them on the prepared baking sheet. Mist the top of the patties with vegetable oil or brush with aquafaba.

5. Bake for 8 minutes, then flip the patties, mist the tops with vegetable oil or brush with aquafaba, and bake for 8 minutes more.

INGREDIENT TIP: In chapter 8, I share a few ways to create plant-based "eggs" at home. One way is by using aquafaba, the liquid from canned or cooked chickpeas, which makes an appearance here as a stand-in for egg wash. I save the aquafaba every time I open a can of chickpeas (or pressure cook dried chickpeas for at least 1 hour). I pour 3 tablespoons of the aquafaba into each well of a silicone ice cube tray, freeze, transfer the cubes to an airtight container, and store them in the freezer for up to 3 months. When I need an "egg" for something, I simply thaw one cube of aquafaba.

PER SERVING (1 PATTY): Calories: 113; Saturated Fat: 1g; Total Fat: 6g; Protein: 11g; Total Carbs: 6g; Fiber: 0g; Sodium: 6mg

INDIAN-STYLE LENTIL AND POTATO HASH

PREP TIME: 10 minutes | **COOK TIME:** 15 minutes | **SERVES:** 4 | Gluten-free, Nut-free option, Soy-free | One-pot, Quick

Potatoes are such a comforting breakfast food, and contrary to food myths, they are super nutritious—low in calories and rich in vitamins C and B$_6$, potassium, and iron. Spuds are typically fried for breakfast, but here they're simmered in a spicy sauce to create a deep, warming flavor. The last-minute addition of lentils contributes even more potassium, plus iron and protein. For a third burst of nutrients, serve over raw or steamed greens.

¼ cup **Vegetable Broth** (page 180) **or water, plus more if needed**

1 **(10-ounce) russet potato, unpeeled, cut into ¼-inch pieces**

1 **teaspoon ground cumin**

½ **teaspoon ground allspice**

½ **teaspoon ground ginger**

½ **teaspoon garam masala**

½ **teaspoon salt or Spicy Umami Blend** (page 196; optional)

1 **(15-ounce) can brown lentils, drained and rinsed**

½ **cup chopped green onions**

½ **cup chopped fresh cilantro** (optional)

¼ **cup chopped peanuts** (optional)

1. In a large skillet, heat the broth over medium-high heat. Add the potato, cumin, allspice, ginger, garam masala, and salt (if using) and cook, stirring frequently, until the potato is tender, about 10 minutes. Add more broth or water as needed to maintain a very thick sauce consistency.

2. Add the lentils and stir to combine. Lower the heat to medium, cover, and cook for 5 minutes more.

3. Divide the lentil mixture among four bowls. Top each serving with 2 tablespoons of green onions, 2 tablespoons of cilantro, and 1 tablespoon of peanuts, then serve.

SWAP IT: You can do a lot of fun things with this recipe. If you love mung beans (I do), use 1½ cups cooked to replace the lentils. Or, for an entirely different flavor profile, use pinto beans and replace the allspice, ginger, and garam masala with 1/2 teaspoon each ground cinnamon, chipotle chile powder, and chili powder.

PER SERVING (1 CUP): Calories: 148; Saturated Fat: 0g; Total Fat: 1g; Protein: 8g; Total Carbs: 29g; Fiber: 7g; Sodium: 28mg

MAPLE MUESLI

PREP TIME: 30 minutes | **COOK TIME:** 20 minutes | **MAKES 5 CUPS** | Gluten-free, Soy-free | 5-ingredient

Millet boasts both protein and magnesium. Dry toasting the millet adds complexity to the overall flavor. Serve this muesli with unsweetened plant-based milk as a breakfast cereal, to top Chocolatey Mousse (page 169), or in a Fruity Yogurt Parfait (page 55).

½ cup dry millet
2 cups rolled oats
1 cup chopped walnuts
½ cup pure maple syrup
1 cup chopped pitted dates

1. Preheat the oven to 350°F. Line a baking sheet with parchment paper or a silicone baking mat.

2. Rinse the millet, drain, and shake off as much water as possible.

3. Heat a medium skillet over medium-high heat.

4. Put the millet in the hot skillet and cook, stirring constantly, until it becomes dry and aromatic and just begins to make popping noises, 5 to 8 minutes. Immediately transfer the millet to a large bowl and let cool for 10 minutes.

5. Add the oats, walnuts, and maple syrup and stir until well combined.

6. Transfer the muesli to the prepared baking sheet and bake for 18 minutes.

7. Place the baking sheet on a wire rack and let cool.

8. Stir in the dates, then transfer the muesli to an airtight container. Store at room temperature for up to 2 weeks.

SWAP IT: If you want to skip the maple syrup, combine the chopped dates and ½ cup boiling water while you toast the millet. Drain the dates, reserving the soaking liquid, and set them aside. Stir the soaking liquid into the oat mixture before baking, then add the dates as directed in the recipe.

PER SERVING (1 CUP): Calories: 515; Saturated Fat: 2g; Total Fat: 18g; Protein: 12g; Total Carbs: 82g; Fiber: 9g; Sodium: 6mg

FRUITY YOGURT PARFAIT

PREP TIME: 5 minutes | **SERVES:** 2 | Gluten-free, Soy-free option | 5-ingredient, No-cook, Quick

I made you work hard for that muesli. Now let's use it for those mornings when you're way too rushed to fuss.

2 cups plain plant-based
  yogurt or **Cashew Cream**
  (page 182)
2 cups fresh blueberries or
  raspberries
1 cup **Maple Muesli**
  (page 54) **or granola**
¼ teaspoon ground
  cinnamon

1. In an individual serving bowl or parfait glass, layer ½ cup of yogurt, 1 cup of berries, ½ cup of muesli, another ½ cup of yogurt, and ⅛ teaspoon of cinnamon.

2. Repeat in a second serving bowl or parfait glass.

SWAP IT: Though I love this parfait with berries, you can make it with seasonal fruits. Cubed watermelon or cantaloupe is terrific in the spring and summer, and diced apple is divine in the fall.

ALLERGEN TIP: For a soy-free parfait, use cashew or almond yogurt.

PER SERVING (2½ CUPS): Calories: 520; Saturated Fat: 2g; Total Fat: 30g; Protein: 14g; Total Carbs: 71g; Fiber: 19g; Sodium: 66mg

APPLE AVOCADO TOAST

PREP TIME: 5 minutes │ **COOK TIME:** 2 minutes │ **SERVES:** 4 │ Soy-free │ No-cook, Quick

Ah, avocado toast. People seem to love it or hate it. I'm on Team Love—there's just something about fresh, thick avocado mashed onto a crisp piece of good bread that makes me feel good. This version is more like a fruit-and-nut guacamole (it would be *great* on homemade corn chips) loaded with contrasting texture and flavors. For a more savory slant, opt for a tart Granny Smith apple. Sweeter? Go with Honey Crisp.

1 large ripe avocado, halved
  and pitted
1 small apple, cored
2 tablespoons lemon juice
½ cup chopped pecans
½ teaspoon ground
  cinnamon
4 slices whole-grain
  bread, toasted

1. Scoop the avocado into a small bowl and mash it with a fork.

2. Cut the apple into ⅛-inch cubes and add it to the avocado.

3. Add the lemon juice, pecans, and cinnamon and gently fold with a rubber spatula until well combined.

4. Spread about ¼ cup of the apple-avocado mixture onto each slice of toast and serve.

CHANGE IT UP: Make this quick breakfast a no-cook one, too. Peel fresh jicama and cut it into sticks (or buy pre-cut jicama sticks at the grocery store), omit the whole-grain toast, and use the apple-avocado mixture as a dip for the jicama.

PER SERVING (¼ CUP APPLE-AVOCADO MIXTURE AND 1 SLICE OF BREAD): Calories: 276; Saturated Fat: 3g; Total Fat: 19g; Protein: 7g; Total Carbs: 25g; Fiber: 9g; Sodium: 101mg

BANANA-NUT BUTTER BOATS

PREP TIME: 5 minutes | **COOK TIME:** 5 minutes | **SERVES:** 2 | Gluten-free, Nut-free option, Soy-free option | 5-ingredient, Quick

I love fruit for breakfast. Fresh, chopped up, and served with walnuts is all I need. But sometimes elevating the fruit can take breakfast to the next level. Cooking bananas brings out the natural sugars and a hint of caramelization and—good news—the heat doesn't diminish the effects of the potassium. Better news? The addition of the protein-packed peanut sauce turns this into a devilishly delicious breakfast.

4 large bananas

½ cup natural or homemade peanut butter

1 tablespoon unsweetened cocoa powder

1 to 2 tablespoons unsweetened soy milk

¼ teaspoon ground cinnamon

1. Peel the bananas and cut them in half lengthwise.

2. In a food processor or blender, combine the peanut butter, cocoa powder, and 1 tablespoon of soy milk and process until thick but easy to pour. Add more soy milk, if needed, to get the right consistency. Set aside.

3. Heat a large skillet over medium-high heat. When a few drops of water quickly bubble up on the surface, place the banana halves cut-side down in the skillet and cook for 1 minute, then turn and cook for 1 minute more.

4. Place 4 banana halves on each of two plates, cut-side up. Drizzle about half the sauce over each plate. Sprinkle a pinch or two of ground cinnamon over each plate and serve.

ALLERGEN TIP: For a nut-free version, try sunflower seed butter. It's delicious. For a soy-free version, use pea milk or a seed-based milk.

PER SERVING (2 BANANAS AND ⅓ CUP SAUCE): Calories: 635; Saturated Fat: 7g; Total Fat: 34g; Protein: 18g; Total Carbs: 78g; Fiber: 11g; Sodium: 14mg

GOLDEN PORRIDGE

PREP TIME: 5 minutes | **COOK TIME:** 1 hour | **SERVES:** 4 | Nut-free option | One-pot

Farro is an unsung breakfast hero. With twice the fiber and protein of traditional wheat, this hardworking grain is a great addition to a morning meal. Naturally nutty with just a hint of cinnamon, the chewy texture of farro contrasts with the sticky rice and cooked vegetables to create an interesting nod to the macrobiotic breakfast bowl. While the soy sauce is optional, you'll likely need a little something to make this porridge pop. If you skip it, be sure to use a little fresh lemon or lime juice.

½ cup dry short-grain brown rice, rinsed and drained

½ cup dry farro, rinsed and drained

1 teaspoon ground turmeric

½ cup fresh or thawed frozen corn

4 cups loosely packed shredded collard greens

¼ cup unsweetened plant-based milk

1 to 2 teaspoons low-sodium soy sauce or tamari (optional)

2 teaspoons sesame seeds

1. In a large saucepan, combine the rice, farro, and 2 cups water and bring to a boil over medium-high heat. Lower the heat to low, cover, and simmer until the rice is tender and the farro is just chewy, 45 to 50 minutes. Remove from the heat.

2. Add the turmeric, corn, and collard greens to the grains and stir gently with a fork to combine. Cover and let sit for 15 minutes.

3. Return the saucepan to medium-low heat. Add the milk and soy sauce (if using) and cook, stirring frequently, until thick and creamy, about 5 minutes.

4. Spoon the porridge into bowls, garnish with the sesame seeds, and serve.

APPLIANCE TIP: To cook this porridge in an Instant Pot or electric pressure cooker, combine all the ingredients except the soy sauce or tamari and the sesame seeds in the pot, lock on the lid, and cook on high pressure for 20 minutes. Allow the pressure to release naturally, then remove the lid, fluff the porridge with a fork while stirring in the soy sauce or tamari, and serve garnished with the sesame seeds.

PER SERVING (1 CUP): Calories: 197; Saturated Fat: 0g; Total Fat: 2g; Protein: 7g; Total Carbs: 40g; Fiber: 5g; Sodium: 60mg

MACRO MISO BREAKFAST SOUP

PREP TIME: 10 minutes | **COOK TIME:** 10 minutes | **SERVES:** 4 | Gluten-free, Nut-free | Quick

Climb aboard the macrobiotic train and try this recipe, which may be mistaken for lunch or dinner but is really meant for breakfast. To shake any doubt out of your head, just think about other savory dishes you enjoy in the morning: hash, scrambles, casseroles. So why not eat soup? This soup begins with vegan dashi—a broth made with kombu (dried kelp)—and calcium-rich bok choy.

1 (3-inch) piece kombu

1 large carrot, unpeeled, chopped (about ½ cup)

1 large celery stalk, chopped (about ½ cup)

1 small sweet potato, unpeeled, cut into ½-inch cubes (about 1 cup)

2 teaspoons ground ginger

8 ounces baby bok choy, halved lengthwise and coarsely chopped

¼ cup red miso paste

1 tablespoon rice vinegar

1. In a large saucepan, combine the kombu and 4 cups water and bring to a boil over medium-high heat. Lower the heat to medium, cover, and cook for 1 minute. Remove the kombu, set aside, and pour the broth into a large measuring cup.

2. Pour about ¼ cup of broth back into the saucepan and heat over medium-high heat. Add the carrot, celery, sweet potato, and ginger and cook, stirring frequently, until the sweet potato is fork-tender, about 5 minutes.

3. Pour the remaining broth into the saucepan and bring to a boil. Add the bok choy, lower the heat to medium, and cook until wilted, about 3 minutes.

4. Remove the saucepan from the heat. Spoon about 1 cup of broth into a bowl or measuring cup. Add the miso to the cup of broth and whisk until dissolved. Pour the miso broth back into the pan, add the vinegar, and stir to combine.

5. Ladle into bowls and serve.

INGREDIENT TIP: Wakame is the edible seaweed you're likely used to seeing in miso soup at restaurants. You can use it in place of the kombu.

PER SERVING (1½ CUPS): Calories: 103; Saturated Fat: 0g; Total Fat: 1g; Protein: 4g; Total Carbs: 18g; Fiber: 4g; Sodium: 643mg

TAHINI BRAISED GREENS

PREP TIME: 5 minutes | **COOK TIME:** 15 minutes | **SERVES:** 2 | Gluten-free, Nut-free, Soy-free | Quick

Let's put an umami cooking technique to work. Braising is a process of frying, then stewing to create rich, complex flavor. This recipe doesn't use oil, so while it's not quite frying, the high heat creates a bit of depth. The addition of rice vinegar and tahini ensures a fifth-flavor bomb. These tahini braised greens are fantastic with Turmeric Tofu Scramble (page 49) for a hearty weekend brunch.

2 tablespoons tahini

2 teaspoons rice vinegar

1 small onion, halved
   and sliced

3 garlic cloves, minced

¾ cup Vegetable Broth
   (page 180)

1 pound kale or Swiss chard,
   leaves stemmed and cut
   into 2-inch pieces

1. Whisk the tahini and vinegar together in a measuring cup or small bowl. Set aside.

2. Heat a large skillet over high heat. Add the onion and garlic, lower the heat to medium-high heat, and cook for about 1 minute. (Add a teaspoon or two of broth if it begins to stick.)

3. Add the greens and cook for 1 minute. Add the broth and tahini-vinegar mixture and stir to combine. Lower the heat to medium, cover, and cook until the greens are soft, about 10 minutes, then serve.

SWAP IT: No tahini? No problem! Use natural sunflower seed butter or peanut butter instead.

PER SERVING (2 CUPS): Calories: 154; Saturated Fat: 1g; Total Fat: 9g; Protein: 7g; Total Carbs: 16g; Fiber: 6g; Sodium: 461mg

GO-TO GRITS

PREP TIME: 5 minutes | **COOK TIME:** 20 minutes | **SERVES:** 4 | Gluten-free, Nut-free, Soy-free | 5-ingredient, One-pot, Quick

Grits might not scream "healthy," but you haven't had these. This piping-hot bowl reminiscent of the Cream of Wheat you might have enjoyed back in the day is a wee bit different. Cornmeal is the grain of choice, and it just happens to be a good source of protein, potassium, and magnesium. No butter is required to make this recipe tasty, because the wonder combo of nutritional yeast and lemon juice gives the grits creaminess and zing. Eat it exactly as is or spoon roasted vegetables over the top for a fun twist on a hippie bowl.

1 cup cornmeal

¼ cup nutritional yeast

2 tablespoons lemon juice

½ teaspoon salt, or
  1 teaspoon Spicy Umami Blend (page 196)

1. In a large saucepan, bring 4 cups water to a boil over high heat.

2. Lower the heat to medium-high and slowly whisk in the cornmeal. Cook, stirring continuously, until it thickens, about 15 minutes.

3. Stir in the nutritional yeast, lemon juice, and salt.

4. Serve immediately.

MAKE AHEAD: Turn these grits into polenta: Line an 8-inch square baking pan with parchment paper. When the grits have finished cooking, immediately pour them into the prepared pan and let cool completely. Cut the polenta into 9 squares and bake in a preheated 400°F oven for 15 to 20 minutes, until heated through.

PER SERVING (1 CUP): Calories: 127; Saturated Fat: 1g; Total Fat: 1g; Protein: 5g; Total Carbs: 25g; Fiber: 2g; Sodium: 156mg

OATMEAL-RAISIN BREAKFAST BOWL

PREP TIME: 5 minutes | **COOK TIME:** 30 minutes | **SERVES:** 4 | Gluten-free, Nut-free option, Soy-free option | One-pot

Here is a more traditional breakfast, but it smells like cookies—how great is that? Cooking these oats with plant-based milk creates a creamy texture. Oatmeal is already easy to cook, but to make it even easier and quicker, use an Instant Pot or other multicooker with a pressure-cooking function. Just increase the plant-based milk to 3 cups and cook on high pressure for 5 minutes, then use a natural pressure release.

1 cup steel-cut oats

2 cups unsweetened plant-based milk

½ cup raisins

1 teaspoon ground cinnamon

¼ cup chopped pitted dates

¼ cup chopped pecans

1. In a large saucepan, combine the oats, milk, raisins, and cinnamon and bring to a boil over medium-high heat.

2. Lower the heat to low and simmer, stirring occasionally, until the oats are tender, about 25 minutes.

3. Remove from the heat. Stir in the dates and pecans, and serve.

SWAP IT: The dates provide just enough sweetness to omit the need for any additional sugar. If you want to skip the dates, any dried fruit will do—I'm partial to dried cherries sweetened with apple juice—or try cacao nibs or shredded coconut for a different flavor.

ALLERGEN TIP: To make this nut-free, omit the pecans and try sunflower seeds instead.

PER SERVING: Calories: 355; Saturated Fat: 1g; Total Fat: 9g; Protein: 10g; Total Carbs: 61g; Fiber: 7g; Sodium: 64mg

SPICY SAVORY OATS

PREP TIME: 10 minutes | **COOK TIME:** 30 minutes | **SERVES:** 4 | Gluten-free, Nut-free,
Soy-free | One-pot

Steel-cut oats are the least-processed oat option, which is a nutritional plus. This version is savory. Just a few tweaks—using vegetable broth instead of plant-based milk, and spicy peppers instead of sweet fruit—transform it into a mainstay breakfast. These oats are great for lunch and dinner, too.

1 large jalapeño, seeded
    and minced, divided
1 small yellow onion, diced
1 large red bell pepper,
    seeded and diced
1 cup steel-cut oats
2 cups Vegetable Broth
    (page 180)
2 tablespoons
    nutritional yeast
½ teaspoon salt, or
    1 teaspoon Spicy Umami
    Blend (page 196)
8 ounces fresh baby spinach
1 large tomato, chopped
1 teaspoon lemon juice

1. In a large saucepan, dry sauté half the jalapeño, the onion, and the bell pepper over medium-high heat for 5 minutes.

2. Add the oats and broth and bring to a boil.

3. Lower the heat to low and simmer, stirring occasionally, until the oats are tender, about 25 minutes. Remove from the heat.

4. Stir in the nutritional yeast, salt, and spinach, cover, and let sit for 5 minutes.

5. In a small bowl, mix together the tomato, remaining jalapeño, and lemon juice.

6. Serve the savory oats with a couple of tablespoons of the salsa over the top.

MAKE AHEAD: Savory oats are great for cooking ahead of time in large batches. Double the recipe, portion out 1-cup servings into airtight containers, and refrigerate for up to 5 days. You'll have plenty to reheat and eat all week long.

PER SERVING: Calories: 202; Saturated Fat: 0g; Total Fat: 2g; Protein: 8g; Total Carbs: 39g; Fiber: 7g; Sodium: 50mg

CHEESY JACKFRUIT CHILAQUILES

PREP TIME: 5 minutes | **COOK TIME:** 20 minutes | **SERVES:** 4 | Gluten-free, Nut-free, Soy-free | Quick

I fell in love with traditional chilaquiles while on vacation in Puerta Vallarta, but I never found a great vegan version. Then I had a happy accident in the kitchen. I was making a quickie enchilada sauce and had just whipped up some homemade tortilla chips in the air fryer. I dipped a chip in the sauce and it was delicious. I like using jackfruit for a plant-based version of "pork" and Cheesy Chickpea Sauce (page 194) for a protein boost.

4 (6-inch) corn tortillas, each cut into 8 strips

3 tablespoons aquafaba (see page 178)

1 (14.5-ounce) can diced tomatoes

1 cup Vegetable Broth (page 180)

4 garlic cloves

1 teaspoon chili powder

1 teaspoon cayenne pepper

1 teaspoon ground cumin

1 teaspoon dried Mexican oregano

1 (14-ounce) can jackfruit, drained

1 cup Cheesy Chickpea Sauce (page 194)

1. Preheat the oven to 350°F. Line a baking sheet with parchment paper or a silicone baking mat.

2. In a bowl, combine the tortillas and aquafaba and toss until the strips are completely coated. Place the tortillas in a single layer on the prepared baking sheet and bake for 15 minutes.

3. In a blender, combine the tomatoes, broth, chili powder, cayenne pepper, cumin, and oregano and purée. Pour the mixture into a large skillet and bring to a boil over medium-high heat. Add the jackfruit to the sauce and return the sauce to a boil. Lower the heat to medium. Add the tortilla strips, gently stir until coated, cover, and cook until the tortillas are slightly soft but still crunchy, 2 to 3 minutes more.

4. Spoon into four bowls. Drizzle about ½ cup of the chickpea sauce over each bowl, if desired, and serve.

SWAP IT: I love the Cheesy Chickpea Sauce because it's a protein *and* flavor boost, but it's completely optional. A simple garnish of chopped green onions, fresh cilantro, and the juice of one lime is fresh and delightful, too.

PER SERVING (2 CUPS): Calories: 253; Saturated Fat: 0g; Total Fat: 3g; Protein: 8g; Total Carbs: 52g; Fiber: 8g; Sodium: 315mg

CHAPTER 5

SALADS AND HANDHELDS

CORN COBB SALAD

PREP TIME: 15 minutes | **COOK TIME:** 20 minutes | **SERVES:** 4 | Gluten-free option, Nut-free

Another cliché about plant-based eating is that it's nothing but salads. But I'm here to tell you that salads are delicious, and they can be filling, too. One way to add more salad to your diet—or to entice reluctant family members to join in—is to play around with the classics. Here, I'm using steamed potatoes, green onion, and wholesome tempeh to replace traditional Cobb items like hard-boiled egg, blue cheese crumbles, and bacon.

6 fingerling potatoes,
unpeeled, cut in half

2 ears corn, shucked and
halved crosswise

½ cup red wine vinegar

¼ cup raw hulled
pumpkin seeds

3 green onions, chopped

1 head Bibb
lettuce, chopped

1 head romaine
lettuce, chopped

½ teaspoon ground
turmeric

½ teaspoon freshly ground
black pepper

¼ teaspoon black salt
(see Tip)

4 pieces Tempeh "Bacon"
(page 183) **chopped**

1. Fill a large saucepan with about 2 inches of water, insert a steamer basket, and bring to a boil over high heat. Lower the heat to medium-high and place the potatoes in the steamer. Cover and steam for 10 minutes.

2. Add the corn to the steamer, cover, and steam for 5 minutes more.

3. While the potatoes and corn are steaming, in a small bowl, mix together the vinegar, pumpkin seeds, and green onions to make a dressing. Set aside.

4. In a large bowl, toss together the chopped lettuces. Set aside.

5. Transfer the corn to a wire rack and let cool. Transfer the potatoes to a medium bowl, and add the turmeric, pepper, and black salt. Stir until the potatoes are evenly coated. Set aside.

6. Pour the dressing over the lettuce and gently toss.

7. Portion the lettuce into four large bowls. Place one piece of corn in the middle of each bowl. Line three pieces of potato along one side of each bowl and sprinkle the tempeh bacon along the other side. Serve.

INGREDIENT TIP: Black salt, also known as kala namak, is sometimes a grayish pink. It contains sulfuric compounds that lend a pleasant eggy flavor, and it's a staple in my cupboard.

ALLERGEN TIP: To make it gluten-free, use a store-bought gluten-free tempeh bacon.

PER SERVING (2 CUPS): Calories: 357; Saturated Fat: 1g; Total Fat: 8g; Protein: 16g; Total Carbs: 59g; Fiber: 11g; Sodium: 86mg

THE WALDORF SALAD

PREP TIME: 10 minutes | **SERVES:** 4 | Gluten-free, Soy-free option | No-cook, Quick

Unsweetened plant-based yogurt makes this fruit-and-veggie-forward salad vegan. Zesting the lemon is optional because you may opt to use bottled juice for ease. But using a fresh lemon adds a natural essential oil, a strong aroma, and a zippy flavor to the salad, so I recommend it. No zester? A box grater will do just fine.

½ cup Tofu Sour Cream
  (page 181)
3 tablespoons lemon juice
2 tablespoons
  nutritional yeast
2 garlic cloves, minced
1 Medjool date, pitted
  (optional)
½ cup chopped walnuts
Zest of 1 lemon (optional)
2 large Honey Crisp or Gala
  apples, cored and cut into
  ¼-inch pieces
2 celery stalks, cut into
  ½-inch pieces
1 cup grapes (any
  kind), halved
1 head red-leaf lettuce,
  chopped or torn into
  bite-size pieces
1 head Bibb or Boston
  lettuce, chopped or torn
  into bite-size pieces

1. In a blender or food processor, combine the sour cream, lemon juice, nutritional yeast, garlic, and date and purée until creamy and pourable. Add 1 to 2 tablespoons of water, if necessary, to make it thinner. Set aside.

2. In a small bowl, combine the walnuts and lemon zest (if using).

3. In a large bowl, combine the apples, celery, and grapes. Add the lettuces and toss to combine. Pour the dressing over the salad and toss until evenly coated.

4. Portion the salad into four bowls. Sprinkle 2 tablespoons of the walnut–lemon zest mixture over each salad and serve.

SWAP IT: I use a Medjool date to add a hint of sweetness, which balances the tangy sour cream, but any type of date or dried fruit will do.

ALLERGEN TIP: To make this soy-free, use plain pea or coconut yogurt.

PER SERVING (1 CUP): Calories: 255; Saturated Fat: 1g; Total Fat: 12g; Protein: 9g; Total Carbs: 34g; Fiber: 6g; Sodium: 45mg

CLASSIC WEDGE SALAD

PREP TIME: 15 minutes | **SERVES:** 4 | Gluten-free option | No-cook, Quick

Iceberg seems to be the poor, forgotten child in the lettuce family. Sure, it may not boast the nutrients that other leafy greens do, but here it plays an important role: to stand tall and strong and hold up an amazing dressing. A traditional wedge salad usually includes crumbled bacon and a blue cheese dressing, but this version marinates raw carrots in a soy-maple sauce and blends avocados with sharp vinegar and a little nutritional yeast to achieve the ultimate flavor and texture.

2 carrots, finely diced

2 tablespoons low-sodium
   soy sauce or tamari

2 teaspoons pure
   maple syrup

½ teaspoon smoked paprika

2 ripe avocados

¼ cup cashews

2 tablespoons apple
   cider vinegar

1 tablespoon
   nutritional yeast

1 teaspoon spirulina powder
   (optional)

1 small red onion, sliced

1 cup cherry or grape
   tomatoes, halved

1 head iceberg lettuce, cut
   into 4 wedges

Freshly ground black pepper

1. Place the carrots a small bowl and let sit for 10 minutes.

2. In a measuring cup, whisk together the soy sauce, maple syrup, and paprika and pour it over the carrots. Set aside.

3. Cut the avocados in half and remove the pits. Dice the flesh of one of the avocado halves in the peel, then gently scoop it out into a small bowl. Set aside.

4. Scoop the flesh from the 3 remaining avocado halves into a blender. Add the cashews, vinegar, nutritional yeast, and spirulina (if using) and purée until very smooth, creamy, and pourable. Add 1 to 2 tablespoons water, if necessary, to reach the right consistency. Pour the dressing into a medium bowl.

5. Add the onion, tomatoes, and carrots (along with the liquid in the bowl) to the bowl with the dressing and stir to combine. Gently fold the diced avocado into the dressing.

6. Place a wedge of lettuce on each of four salad plates. Dress the lettuce by spooning about ½ cup of dressing over each wedge, then repeat until the dressing is used up. Sprinkle a pinch or two of black pepper over each salad and serve.

SWAP IT: The carrot bits make this a quick, no-cook salad, but you can easily use crumbled Tempeh "Bacon" (page 183). Lightlife and Tofurky also make minimally processed packaged tempeh bacon.

ALLERGEN TIP: If you are sensitive to gluten, be sure to use tamari labeled "gluten-free" or coconut aminos.

PER SERVING (1 WEDGE): Calories: 298; Saturated Fat: 4g; Total Fat: 20g; Protein: 8g; Total Carbs: 29g; Fiber: 13g; Sodium: 303mg

CHEF SALAD

PREP TIME: 15 minutes | **COOK TIME:** 15 minutes | **SERVES:** 4 | Gluten-free, Nut-free | Quick

For this chef salad, I didn't want to get literal and make "ham" when instead I could use other flavors I enjoyed from the original salad—like the sweet pineapple garnish and smoky red paprika—and build complexity in a far healthier way. Tomato powder is simply ground dehydrated tomatoes; it adds color and a pop of flavor.

6 fingerling potatoes, unpeeled, cut in half

2 teaspoons smoked paprika, divided

½ teaspoon ground turmeric

½ teaspoon freshly ground black pepper

¼ teaspoon black salt (see Tip, page 69)

2 cups fresh or drained canned pineapple chunks

1 small cucumber, unpeeled, cut into ¼-inch dice

1 tablespoon rice vinegar

6 ounces silken tofu

1 tablespoon lime juice

2 garlic cloves, peeled

2 teaspoons tomato powder

2 heads romaine lettuce, chopped

1. Fill a large saucepan with about 2 inches of water, insert a steamer basket, and bring to a boil over high heat. Lower the heat to medium-high and place the potatoes in the steamer. Cover and steam for 15 minutes. Transfer the potatoes to a small bowl, sprinkle with 1 teaspoon of paprika, the turmeric, pepper, and black salt and toss until evenly coated. Place in the refrigerator to chill.

2. In a small bowl, combine the pineapple and remaining 1 teaspoon of paprika until evenly coated. Set aside.

3. In another small bowl, combine the cucumber and vinegar. Set aside.

4. In a food processor or blender, combine the tofu, lime juice, garlic, and tomato powder and purée until thick and creamy. Remove the food processor blade, add the cucumber-vinegar mixture, and stir to combine.

5. Place the lettuce in a large bowl. Pour the tofu dressing over the lettuce and toss until evenly coated.

6. Portion the salad into four large salad bowls. Top each bowl with three pieces of potato and ½ cup of pineapple mixture, then serve.

MAKE AHEAD: Complete steps 1 through 3 in advance, cover each bowl, and chill for up to 3 days. This will create even deeper flavors.

PER SERVING (2 TO 3 CUPS): Calories: 219; Saturated Fat: 1g; Total Fat: 4g; Protein: 11g; Total Carbs: 43g; Fiber: 11g; Sodium: 126mg

CAPER CAESAR SALAD

PREP TIME: 10 minutes | **SERVES:** 4 | Gluten-free, Soy-free | No-cook, Quick

Pickled and fermented veggies can turn any ho-hum salad into something extra-special, because that's how umami (see page 15) works. For this twist on a classic, I'm not doing anything crazy. Adding a small amount of briny capers simply turns this into a taste bud dance party. No capers? Try a blend of chopped pitted green, Greek, and black olives.

½ cup plus 1 tablespoon raw cashews, divided

2 heads romaine lettuce, chopped

2 tablespoons Boozy Brown Mustard (page 188) or Dijon mustard

3 tablespoons lemon juice

1 tablespoon capers, drained

2 garlic cloves, minced

1 Medjool date, pitted

1 teaspoon Spicy Umami Blend (page 196), or ½ teaspoon kosher salt

½ teaspoon ground white pepper

¼ cup hemp seeds

1. Place ½ cup of cashews in a measuring cup and add hot water to cover. Set aside to soak for 30 minutes.

2. Place the lettuce in a large bowl. Set aside.

3. Drain the cashews and transfer them to a blender. Add the mustard, lemon juice, capers, garlic, date, umami blend, and white pepper and purée until creamy and pourable. Add more lemon juice or water, if necessary, to make it thinner.

4. Pour the dressing over the lettuce and toss until evenly coated.

5. Chop the remaining 1 tablespoon of cashews and combine with the hemp seeds in a small bowl. Sprinkle the cashew mixture over the lettuce and gently stir to combine.

6. Portion the salad into four bowls and serve.

SMART SHOPPING: Capers can usually be found in two places at your local grocer: jarred in the condiment aisle, or near the salad bar in the deli, where you can buy olives in bulk. I prefer the jarred variety because they are cost-effective and last a long time in the refrigerator.

PER SERVING (3 CUPS): Calories: 235; Saturated Fat: 2g; Total Fat: 14g; Protein: 9g; Total Carbs: 24g; Fiber: 9g; Sodium: 310mg

JACKFRUIT LOUIE AVOCADO SALAD

PREP TIME: 15 minutes | **SERVES:** 4 | Gluten-free, Nut-free | No-cook, Quick

Jackfruit is your plant-based go-to when you're looking for meaty texture. It can stand in for shredded pork in sandwiches or enchiladas, and it's a great vegan version of crabmeat. Tangy sour cream gets a little smoky with spices to create a Worcestershire-style flavor. You can turn this meal into an appetizer by increasing the number of avocados to 4, halving and pitting them, and putting a little dollop of the jackfruit Louie in the center.

½ cup Tofu Sour Cream
  (page 181)
2 teaspoons apple
  cider vinegar
1 garlic clove, minced
¼ teaspoon ground ginger
¼ teaspoon
  ground mustard
¼ teaspoon onion powder
1 (14-ounce) can
  jackfruit, drained
1 teaspoon chili powder
8 cups chopped lettuce
2 ripe avocados, halved
  and pitted

1. In a small bowl, whisk together the sour cream, vinegar, garlic, ginger, ground mustard, and onion powder. Set aside.

2. Place the jackfruit in a medium bowl. Dust with the chili powder and stir until evenly coated. Add the sour cream mixture and stir to combine. Set aside.

3. Plate 2 cups of the chopped lettuce on each of four salad plates. Scoop the flesh from 1 avocado half over the lettuce on each plate. Spoon ½ cup of the jackfruit mixture into each avocado half. Spoon the remaining jackfruit mixture equally over each plate and serve.

SMART SHOPPING: If you use jackfruit frequently, visit your local Asian or international grocer, where you can buy it fresh (beware—peeling a fresh jackfruit is a lot of work) or canned, and in bulk.

PER SERVING: Calories: 337; Saturated Fat: 3g; Total Fat: 18g; Protein: 11g; Total Carbs: 39g; Fiber: 12g; Sodium: 47mg

ARTICHOKE TUNA-ISH SALAD

PREP TIME: 10 minutes, plus 30 minutes chilling | **SERVES:** 4 | Gluten-free, Nut-free | No-cook

This super-fast and super-simple salad packs a ton of flavor, thanks to briny artichoke hearts. Artichokes are packed with fiber and vitamin C, which is why I always have plenty on hand, both canned and frozen. Dulse (a type of seaweed) brings in the flavor and aroma. Serve this salad on a whole-grain wrap or collard green leaf, or toss it with chopped lettuce.

2 (14-ounce) cans quartered artichoke hearts, drained

½ cup Tofu Sour Cream (page 181)

½ cup diced sweet onion

½ cup diced celery

1 teaspoon dulse flakes, or 1 teaspoon Spicy Umami Blend (page 196)

1. Coarsely chop the artichoke hearts and transfer them to a medium bowl.

2. Add the sour cream, onion, celery, and dulse and stir to combine.

3. Cover the bowl or transfer the mixture to an airtight container and refrigerate for at least 30 minutes or up to 3 days before serving.

INGREDIENT TIP: If you'd prefer to use fresh or frozen artichoke hearts, soak them in 2 tablespoons rice vinegar in the refrigerator for at least 1 hour or up to overnight to give them a briny flavor.

SWAP IT: Use plain plant-based yogurt instead of the Tofu Sour Cream.

PER SERVING (1½ CUPS): Calories: 157; Saturated Fat: 0g; Total Fat: 3g; Protein: 10g; Total Carbs: 27g; Fiber: 18g; Sodium: 147mg

CHICK(PEA) PECAN SALAD

PREP TIME: 5 minutes | **SERVES:** 4 | Gluten-free, Soy-free | No-cook, Quick

This is a super-fresh take on the traditionally heavy chicken pecan salad. This salad, which involves just a light-handed pour of vinegar over chickpeas and vegetables, is great on a slice of crusty whole-grain bread. For a completely veg-centric approach, try stuffing this salad into a hollowed-out large tomato or bell pepper.

1 (15-ounce) can chickpeas, drained and rinsed

1 (4-ounce) jar hearts of palm, drained

½ teaspoon ground thyme

½ teaspoon ground sage

1 large celery stalk, chopped

¼ cup dried cranberries

2 tablespoons rice vinegar

¼ cup chopped pecans

1. Place the chickpeas and hearts of palm in a food processor and pulse in 1-second bursts until the mixture has a flaky texture. Be careful not to overprocess. Transfer the mixture to a medium bowl.

2. Add the thyme, sage, celery, cranberries, vinegar, and pecans and stir to combine.

3. Serve immediately, or store in an airtight container in the refrigerator for up to 5 days.

SMART SHOPPING: Hearts of palm are briny, and an opened jar can be stored in the refrigerator for months. Consider going to a warehouse store like Costco or Sam's Club to buy extra-large jars.

PER SERVING (1 CUP): Calories: 225; Saturated Fat: 1g; Total Fat: 7g; Protein: 8g; Total Carbs: 35g; Fiber: 7g; Sodium: 198mg

LOADED POTATO WITH TOFU "EGG" SALAD

PREP TIME: 20 minutes, plus 1 hour chilling | **COOK TIME:** 30 minutes | **SERVES:** 4 | Gluten-free, Nut-free

Tofu is an excellent replacement for eggs because the texture is spot on. Bonus: lots of protein! The ground mustard and black salt provide the color and smell that you would expect from eggs, plus rich flavor. You can skip the potatoes and simply serve the mixture on toasted bread or in a salad.

2 large russet potatoes, unpeeled, scrubbed
1 (14-ounce) package extra-firm tofu, pressed (see page 23) **and drained**
½ cup chopped celery
½ cup chopped red onion
½ cup Tofu Sour Cream (page 181)
1 teaspoon ground mustard
½ teaspoon black salt (see Tip, page 69), **or** 1 teaspoon Spicy Umami Blend (page 196)
¼ teaspoon freshly ground black pepper
½ teaspoon smoked paprika

1. Fill a large saucepan with 1 to 2 inches of water, insert a steamer basket, and bring to a boil over high heat. Lower the heat to medium-high and place the potatoes in the steamer. Cover and steam for 30 minutes, until the potatoes are tender. Transfer the potatoes to a bowl and refrigerate for at least 1 hour or up to 3 days.

2. Place the tofu in a large bowl and gently mash it with a fork or potato masher until crumbled. Add the celery, onion, sour cream, ground mustard, black salt, and pepper and stir until combined. Transfer the mixture to an airtight container and refrigerate for at least 1 hour or up to 3 days.

3. Cut the chilled potatoes in half. Using a spoon, carefully scoop out the flesh, leaving about ½ inch attached to the skins; reserve the flesh for another use.

4. Spoon ¼ to ½ cup of the tofu mixture into each potato skin and sprinkle with paprika, then serve.

INGREDIENT TIP: What to do with the flesh you scoop from the potatoes? Reheat it with a little lemon juice, nutritional yeast, and black pepper for quick (and healthy) mashed potatoes.

PER SERVING (1 CUP): Calories: 287; Saturated Fat: 2g; Total Fat: 8g; Protein: 18g; Total Carbs: 38g; Fiber: 4g; Sodium: 49mg

THREE GRAIN SALAD

PREP TIME: 20 minutes, plus 30 minutes chilling | **COOK TIME:** 50 minutes | **SERVES:** 6 | Soy-free

Wheat berries and barley are rich in fiber, protein, and potassium, and their chewiness makes them a great ground meat alternative in tacos and sloppy joes. Brown rice provides B vitamins. Simplicity delivers!

¼ cup dry wheat berries

¼ cup dry barley

¼ cup dry brown rice

¼ cup Boozy Brown Mustard
(page 188)

1 tablespoon
balsamic vinegar

2 garlic cloves, minced

6 cups finely shredded
Swiss chard leaves

¼ cup chopped unsalted
pistachios

1. Pour 2½ cups water in a large saucepan and bring to a boil over high heat.

2. In a colander, combine the wheat berries, barley, and rice and rinse well. Add the mixed grains to the boiling water, stir, and return the water to a boil. Lower the heat to medium-low, cover tightly, and cook until the grains are fork-tender and slightly chewy, 45 to 50 minutes. Remove from the heat and let sit, covered, for 10 minutes.

3. Using a fork, fluff the grains, lifting and separating them. Transfer the grains to a medium bowl and refrigerate for at least 30 minutes or up to 3 days.

4. In a small bowl, whisk together the mustard, vinegar, and garlic. Use immediately, or store in an airtight container in the refrigerator for up to 2 weeks.

5. To assemble the salad, place the chard in a large bowl. Add the cold cooked grains and the mustard dressing and gently toss. Toss in the pistachios before serving. Store leftovers in an airtight container in the refrigerator for up to 5 days.

SWAP IT: Kale is a great substitute for the chard here. Use 8 cups tightly packed shredded kale leaves. Massage the kale (see page 82) with the dressing and refrigerate, covered, for up to 3 days, leaving out the grains and pistachios until ready to serve.

PER SERVING (1½ CUPS): Calories: 125; Saturated Fat: 0g; Total Fat: 3g; Protein: 4g; Total Carbs: 22g; Fiber: 4g; Sodium: 79mg

MASSAGED KALE SALAD

PREP TIME: 10 minutes | **SERVES:** 4 | Gluten-free, Nut-free, Soy-free | No-cook, Quick

Did you know that to enjoy kale raw, all you need to do is give it a gentle massage with a little fat and acid to break it down and make it easier to eat and digest? When you do, the volume reduces (sometimes by nearly half) and the color becomes a deep green. The addition of hemp seeds creates a texture similar to that of Parmesan, and they cling to the tahini-coated kale leaves. Serve the salad as is or power it up with baked tofu, roasted chickpeas, or Tempeh "Bacon" (page 183).

2 bunches kale, leaves
    stemmed and torn into
    bite-size pieces
¼ cup tahini
¼ cup lemon juice
2 garlic cloves, minced
¼ cup hemp seeds
1 teaspoon salt or Spicy
    Umami Blend (page 196)

1. Place the kale in a large bowl. Add the tahini, lemon juice, and garlic. With clean or gloved hands, massage the kale until it brightens and glistens and the leaves are coated, about 3 minutes.

2. Sprinkle the hemp seeds and salt over the salad and toss gently, then serve.

SWAP IT: Peanut, almond, and sunflower seed butters are all fantastic substitutes for the tahini. Lime or orange juice can be used instead of lemon juice.

PER SERVING (2 CUPS): Calories: 162; Saturated Fat: 2g; Total Fat: 13g; Protein: 6g; Total Carbs: 9g; Fiber: 3g; Sodium: 31mg

SPICY HUMMUS WRAP

PREP TIME: 10 minutes | **SERVES:** 4 | Gluten-free, Soy-free | No-cook, Quick

Come on, you knew a hummus recipe was inevitable! It's just too darn easy and delicious. Seriously, *everyone* should have a go-to recipe for this flavorful bean dip. Here I've played with a za'atar flavor profile to add a little zing. There's some flexibility, too—try cannellini or butter beans, or use peanut or sunflower seed butter instead of almond butter. Add a little texture to this wrap by adding carrot, bell pepper, and/or cucumber sticks.

1 (15-ounce) can chickpeas, drained and rinsed

1 tablespoon natural almond butter

1 teaspoon lemon zest or ground sumac

2 to 3 tablespoons lemon juice

2 garlic cloves, coarsely chopped

1 teaspoon sesame seeds

1 teaspoon nutritional yeast

¼ teaspoon dried thyme

¼ teaspoon dried oregano

4 whole-grain tortillas

4 Swiss or rainbow chard leaves or large lettuce leaves

1. In a food processor, combine the chickpeas, almond butter, lemon zest, lemon juice, garlic, sesame seeds, nutritional yeast, thyme, and oregano and purée until smooth and creamy, adding water 1 teaspoon at a time as needed to achieve the desired consistency.

2. Place the tortillas on a large cutting board. Spread one-quarter of the hummus (about ½ cup) over each. Place one chard or lettuce leaf on top of the hummus. Roll up and serve.

INGREDIENT TIP: Throughout this book when I recommend bread or wraps, I suggest whole-grain. I often turn to sprouted-grain bread products by Ezekiel 4:9. But that's obviously not an option if you're gluten-free, and some of you may want an even healthier alternative to bread. Many interesting minimally processed and vegetable-forward wraps are available at health food and online vegan stores. I recommend checking out WrawP, Angelic Bakehouse, and Raw Wraps.

PER SERVING (1 WRAP): Calories: 287; Saturated Fat: 3g; Total Fat: 9g; Protein: 12g; Total Carbs: 42g; Fiber: 11g; Sodium: 502mg

YELLOW DAL COLLARD WRAPS

PREP TIME: 10 minutes, plus 30 minutes chilling | **COOK TIME:** 20 minutes | **SERVES:** 4 | Gluten-free, Nut-free, Soy-free

Split beans like split peas, red lentils, and these yellow split peas cook up fast with no soaking required. They are creamy and packed with protein, making them an ideal choice for bean dip spreads for nutrient-packed wraps like this one. If raw collard greens aren't your thing, Swiss chard or romaine leaves also work well. For adorable appetizer-size wraps, make "boats" using endive or radicchio leaves.

1 cup chopped carrots

2 garlic cloves, minced

1 teaspoon fennel
  seed, crushed

1 cup dried yellow split
  peas, green split peas, or
  red lentils

2 tablespoons lemon juice

1 tablespoon rice vinegar

1 teaspoon salt or Spicy
  Umami Blend (page 196)

4 large collard green
  leaves, stemmed

2 red bell peppers, seeded
  and cut into 8 long pieces

1. In a large saucepan, combine the carrot and garlic and sauté over medium-high heat, stirring frequently to keep the garlic from sticking, for 3 minutes. Add the fennel, lentils, and 2¼ cups water and bring to a boil. Lower the heat to medium-low, cover, and simmer until the lentils are tender, 15 to 20 minutes.

2. Remove from the heat; add the lemon juice, vinegar, and salt; and mash and stir until thick and creamy. Set aside to cool, then transfer the dal to an airtight container and refrigerate for at least 30 minutes or up to 5 days before using.

3. To make the wraps, place a collard leaf on a cutting board, bright-side down, and spread 1 cup of dal over the leaf. Add 2 bell pepper sticks. Fold one long end of the collard leaf toward the middle. Fold the opposite end toward the middle. Fold the other two sides in toward the middle. Place the wrap on a plate, seam-side down. Repeat with the remaining ingredients.

MAKE AHEAD: Cook the dal in bulk, and give it a couple of days in the refrigerator. It will be the perfect texture to spread over the crispy leafy greens for lunch or dinner.

PER SERVING (1 CUP): Calories: 223; Saturated Fat: 0g; Total Fat: 1g; Protein: 14g; Total Carbs: 41g; Fiber: 16g; Sodium: 330mg

"BACON," ARUGULA, AND AVOCADO SANDWICH

PREP TIME: 15 minutes | **COOK TIME:** 20 minutes | **SERVES:** 2 | Nut-free | 5-ingredient

Here is a super-healthy and fresh approach to a traditional BLT.

Give me a "B" for bacon-style tempeh!
Give me an "A" for peppery arugula to replace lettuce!
Give me another "A" for avocado to replace tomato and stand in for mayo!

1 avocado, halved
   and pitted
4 slices whole-grain
   bread, toasted
1 batch Tempeh "Bacon"
   (page 183)
2 cups loosely
   packed arugula

1. Scoop the avocado into a small bowl and mash it with a fork.

2. Spread one-quarter of the mashed avocado on each slice of bread. Top 2 slices of the bread with 2 pieces of tempeh bacon and 1 cup of arugula each, then add 2 more pieces of tempeh bacon and top with the remaining 2 slices of bread, avocado-side down. Serve.

SWAP IT: Prefer a wrap over toasted bread? Use two big whole-grain tortillas or two large collard leaves.

PER SERVING (1 SANDWICH): Calories: 612; Saturated Fat: 5g; Total Fat: 30g; Protein: 33g; Total Carbs: 59g; Fiber: 13g; Sodium: 365mg

AVOCADO SUSHI ROLLS

PREP TIME: 10 minutes, plus 30 minutes chilling | **SERVES:** 4 | Gluten-free, Nut-free, Soy-free | 5-ingredient

Most people think of fish when sushi is mentioned. But no seafood is required here. Simply use a sheet of nori (a type of seaweed—look for it in the international aisle near the Asian foods at your local grocer), rice, and your favorite veggies. I like avocado for its fat, flavor, and color. Make the brown rice ahead while meal prepping or bulk cooking.

½ cup cold cooked brown rice

1 tablespoon mirin or rice vinegar

1 large date, pitted and finely chopped

1 large avocado, halved and pitted

4 (8-by-7-inch) sheets nori

1. In a bowl, mix together the rice, mirin, and date. Refrigerate for at least 30 minutes.

2. Using the tip of a sharp knife, cut each avocado half into 4 slices. Using a spoon, gently scoop the slices out of the peel and set them aside on a small plate.

3. Place 1 sheet of nori on a cutting board. Spoon 1 tablespoon of rice mixture onto the nori, making a line of rice on the edge closest to you. Add 2 avocado slices on top of the rice.

4. Pull the edge of the nori sheet away from the cutting board and roll it over the filling tightly until the filling is completely enclosed. Repeat with the remaining ingredients.

5. Serve the rolls whole, or cut each into 4 pieces.

SWAP IT: Carrot, cucumber, and bell pepper sticks are all great substitutes for avocado—just be careful not to overfill the nori or it will be hard to roll. Use only one!

PER SERVING (1 SUSHI ROLL): Calories: 124; Saturated Fat: 2g; Total Fat: 8g; Protein: 2g; Total Carbs: 13g; Fiber: 5g; Sodium: 2mg

SPRING ROLLS WITH PISTACHIO SAUCE

PREP TIME: 15 minutes | **SERVES:** 4 | Gluten-free, Soy-free | No-cook, Quick

Rice paper wrappers, also called spring roll skins, are really easy to find; check the international aisle of your local grocery store. I've aimed for simplicity with the vegetables, so the "wow" is in the sauce. Pistachios are an honorary legume and pack a protein punch.

1 large cucumber

1 large carrot

4 ounces fresh basil

½ cup shelled unsalted pistachios

1 serrano pepper or jalapeño, halved and seeded

3 tablespoons rice vinegar

8 rice paper wrappers

1. Cut the cucumber in half crosswise and cut each half into 16 (¼-inch-wide) sticks.

2. Quarter the carrot lengthwise and cut each quarter into 4 (¼-inch-wide) sticks.

3. In a food processor, combine the basil, pistachios, serrano, and vinegar and purée, adding 1 tablespoon water at a time as needed to create a thick sauce.

4. Pour warm water into a shallow bowl. Dip 1 rice paper wrapper into the water until moistened, about 5 seconds (do not let it soak). Place the wrapper on a work surface and let sit until pliable, about 30 seconds. Dollop about 2 tablespoons of the pistachio sauce on the wrapper and add 2 cucumber sticks and 2 carrot sticks. Lift one side of the wrapper and fold it over the filling, tucking it under the filling. Fold in the sides and roll up the spring roll. Repeat with the remaining ingredients.

5. Plate the rolls and drizzle the sauce on top. Store the sauce in an airtight container in the refrigerator for up to 5 days.

INGREDIENT TIP: Use the pistachio sauce as a vegetable dip; dollop it over a bowl of beans, greens, and grains; or spread it over whole-grain toast for an alternative to avocado toast.

PER SERVING (2 SPRING ROLLS): Calories: 202; Saturated Fat: 1g; Total Fat: 7g; Protein: 5g; Total Carbs: 30g; Fiber: 3g; Sodium: 266mg

CREAMY RICED VEGGIE WRAP

PREP TIME: 10 minutes | **SERVES:** 8 | Gluten-free | No-cook, Quick

You've likely heard of cauliflower rice, a low-carb alternative to rice, but I'm here to introduce you to edamame rice. It's the same concept, but edamame is protein-rich (17 grams per cup!) and a significant source of potassium, vitamin C, and even iron and calcium. Plus, it's green and pretty. And that matters, because you're going to create a rainbow of color with very little effort.

2 cups frozen shelled edamame, thawed

1 carrot, unpeeled, coarsely chopped

1 yellow bell pepper, stemmed, seeded, and cut into 4 pieces

½ cup grape tomatoes, halved

½ cup Miso Cream Sauce (page 197)

8 plant wraps of your choice (collard green leaves, chard leaves, or nori sheets)

1. In a food processor, combine the edamame, carrot, and bell pepper and pulse in quick 5-second bursts to break down the vegetables into pieces the size of grains of rice. Transfer to a medium bowl.

2. Add the tomatoes and miso sauce and stir gently to combine.

3. Spoon about ¾ cup of the riced veggies onto the wrap of your choice. Roll them up and eat.

SWAP IT: You can now actually buy frozen cauliflower rice and frozen edamame rice. In a pinch, opt for either of them, thaw, and roll up with carrot or bell pepper sticks and avocado slices.

PER SERVING (1 WRAP): Calories: 69; Saturated Fat: 0g; Total Fat: 3g; Protein: 4g; Total Carbs: 8g; Fiber: 3g; Sodium: 157mg

VEGGIE LUNCH MUFFINS

PREP TIME: 10 minutes | **COOK TIME:** 20 minutes | **MAKES:** 6 muffins | Gluten-free, Soy-free | Quick

Do you ever find yourself running errands over the lunch hour and wishing you had a wholesome on-the-go meal? Or have you yearned for something easy to pack in your kid's backpack for a quick after-school snack? This bean-and-veggie-based "muffin" is easy to make, quick to bake, and perfect for toting around for a boost of nutrition when you have no time to eat.

Vegetable oil spray
(optional)
1 tablespoon ground
flaxseed
3 tablespoons warm water
1 (15-ounce) can cannellini
beans, drained and rinsed
½ cup coconut milk
1 tablespoon
nutritional yeast
1 cup grated zucchini
1 cup finely chopped red
bell pepper
1 cup chopped
fresh spinach
1 teaspoon salt, or
2 teaspoons Spicy Umami
Blend (page 196)

1. Preheat the oven to 375°F. Spray a 6-cup muffin tin (or 6 wells of a standard muffin tin) with vegetable oil or line them with paper liners (or use a nonstick muffin tin).

2. In a small bowl or measuring cup, whisk together the flaxseed and warm water. Set aside.

3. In a food processor, combine the beans, coconut milk, and nutritional yeast and process until smooth and creamy. Transfer the mixture to a large bowl.

4. Add the zucchini, bell pepper, spinach, and salt to the bean mixture and mix well.

5. Using an ice cream scoop or ¼-cup measuring cup, divide the vegetable-bean mixture among the prepared muffin cups.

6. Bake for 20 minutes, until golden brown and a toothpick inserted into the center of a muffin comes out clean.

7. Serve warm, or store in an airtight container at room temperature for up to 3 days or in the refrigerator for up to 5 days.

SWAP IT: Try these with black beans or chickpeas.

PER SERVING (1 MUFFIN): Calories: 122; Saturated Fat: 4g; Total Fat: 5g; Protein: 5g; Total Carbs: 15g; Fiber: 1g; Sodium: 130mg

CHAPTER 6

SOUPS AND STEWS

CLASSIC VEGETABLE SOUP

PREP TIME: 10 minutes | **COOK TIME:** 20 minutes | **SERVES:** 4 to 6 | Gluten-free, No-cook, Nut-free, Soy-free option | One-pot, Quick

Simplicity is underrated. Start with vegetables and spices you *always* have on hand (or will, after reading this book), add a bit of miso paste for—you guessed it—umami (plus a little protein bonus), and you've got yourself a comforting, wholesome soup that I predict will become part of your regular meal-prepping rotation.

1 tablespoon red miso paste

2 cups diced onion

1 cup diced carrots

1 cup diced russet potatoes

3 garlic cloves, minced

½ teaspoon dried basil

½ teaspoon dried oregano

½ teaspoon dried thyme

3 cups Vegetable Broth
  (page 180)

1 cup chopped frozen or
  fresh green beans

1 cup diced tomato

1. In a large saucepan, bring ¼ cup water to a simmer over medium-high heat. Add the miso and whisk until thick and smooth. Add the onion, carrots, potatoes, garlic, basil, oregano, thyme, and broth and bring to a boil. Lower the heat to medium-low, cover, and simmer for 10 minutes.

2. Add the green beans and tomato and bring back to a boil. Lower the heat, cover, and simmer for 5 minutes more, then serve.

ALLERGEN TIP: To make this soy-free, sauté the vegetables with 2 teaspoons Spicy Umami Blend (page 196) instead of the miso paste.

PER SERVING (2 CUPS): Calories: 103; Saturated Fat: 0g; Total Fat: 1g; Protein: 4g; Total Carbs: 23g; Fiber: 4g; Sodium: 190mg

CREAM OF MISO MUSHROOM STEW

PREP TIME: 10 minutes | **COOK TIME:** 15 minutes | **SERVES:** 4 to 6 | Gluten-free option | One-pot, Quick

With just a handful of ingredients, this rich and creamy bowl of soup delivers comfort and unbeatable flavor when you need it. Mushrooms are prominent in plant-based cooking, not only for their nutrients but also for the meatiness and umami they bring to each bite. I love serving this soup with Spring Rolls with Pistachio Sauce (page 89) or Avocado Sushi Rolls (page 87) for an Asian-inspired take on a soup-and-sandwich lunch or dinner.

1 tablespoon low-sodium soy sauce or tamari
1 cup julienned green onions
2 cups sliced mushrooms (shiitake, oyster, or baby bella)
2 cups Miso Cream Sauce (page 197)
2 cups Vegetable Broth (page 180)
1 tablespoon rice vinegar

1. In a large saucepan, heat the soy sauce over medium-high heat. Add the green onions and mushrooms and sauté until tender, 3 to 5 minutes. Add the miso cream sauce and sauté until it begins to thicken, about 3 minutes.

2. Add the broth and bring to a boil. Lower the heat to low and simmer, stirring occasionally, for 10 minutes.

3. Remove from the heat. Stir in the vinegar and serve.

SWAP IT: I call for green onions because they are easy to find, but negi (Japanese leeks), leeks, or bunching onions are great substitutes.

ALLERGEN TIP: Use gluten-free tamari or coconut aminos and be sure to use a gluten-free miso paste in your Miso Cream Sauce.

PER SERVING (1½ CUPS): Calories: 156; Saturated Fat: 1g; Total Fat: 7g; Protein: 8g; Total Carbs: 13g; Fiber: 2g; Sodium: 476mg

CHICKPEA NOODLE SOUP

PREP TIME: 10 minutes | **COOK TIME:** 25 minutes | **SERVES:** 4 to 6 | Nut-free, Soy-free

The first time I got a cold as a vegan, I whined, "I want something like chicken noodle soup!" A quick scan of the cupboard produced two key ingredients: canned chickpeas and a package of never-used soba noodles. I wanted comfort food in a hurry, so I started boiling the noodles and got a quick mirepoix (see page 49) going. It did the job. The more flavorful approach I've used in this recipe is perfect no matter how you're feeling.

4 ounces dried soba noodles

4 cups Vegetable Broth (page 180), **divided**

2 cups diced onions

1 cup chopped carrots

1 cup chopped celery

3 garlic cloves, finely diced

½ teaspoon dried parsley

½ teaspoon dried sage

½ teaspoon dried thyme

½ teaspoon freshly ground black or white pepper

1 (15-ounce) can chickpeas, drained and rinsed

¼ cup chopped fresh parsley, for garnish (optional)

1. In a large saucepan, bring 4 cups water to a boil over high heat. Add the soba noodles and cook, stirring occasionally, until just tender, 4 to 5 minutes. Drain in a colander and rinse well under cold water. Set aside.

2. In the same saucepan, heat ¼ cup of broth over medium-high heat. Add the onions, carrots, celery, garlic, parsley, sage, thyme, and pepper and sauté for 5 minutes, or until the carrots are fork-tender.

3. Add the chickpeas and remaining 3¾ cups of broth and bring to a boil. Lower the heat to low, cover, and simmer for 15 minutes.

4. Serve garnished with the parsley, if desired.

INGREDIENT TIP: I love using soba noodles in Spring Rolls with Pistachio Sauce (page 89) or as a grain addition to a salad. Make an entire package at once, use what you need for this soup, and store the rest in an airtight container in the refrigerator for up to 5 days.

PER SERVING (1 CUP): Calories: 266; Saturated Fat: 0g; Total Fat: 3g; Protein: 12g; Total Carbs: 53g; Fiber: 8g; Sodium: 351mg

TANGY TOMATO SOUP

PREP TIME: 5 minutes | **COOK TIME:** 30 minutes | **SERVES:** 4 | Gluten-free, Nut-free, Soy-free | One-pot

Try flexing your umami muscles with caramelly onions and balsamic vinegar, which take the tomatoes in this simple soup to the next level. Cooking the onions over higher heat creates an aroma and flavor nearing caramelized onions without all the effort, and the subtle sweetness from the date helps balance the acidity of the soup. Serve as is or consider adding a verdant dollop of Plant Pesto (page 185) in the middle of each bowl for a pop of color.

1 large sweet onion, coarsely chopped

1 (28-ounce) can diced tomatoes

1 (28-ounce) can crushed tomatoes

1 cup Vegetable Broth (page 180)

2 teaspoons dried tarragon

1 Medjool date, pitted and chopped (optional)

¼ cup balsamic vinegar

1. In a large saucepan, dry sauté the onion over medium-high heat, stirring frequently, until just beginning to brown, 8 to 10 minutes. Add the diced and crushed tomatoes, broth, and tarragon and bring to a boil.

2. Lower the heat to medium-low and simmer, stirring frequently, for 20 minutes.

3. Add the date and use an immersion blender to purée the soup directly in the pan until smooth (or transfer the soup to a standing blender and carefully purée, then return the soup to the pan).

4. Pour in the vinegar, quickly stir, and serve hot.

SWAP IT: No tarragon? No problem! Use ¼ teaspoon ground fennel seed and ¼ teaspoon ground anise seed.

PER SERVING (2 CUPS): Calories: 153; Saturated Fat: 0g; Total Fat: 1g; Protein: 6g; Total Carbs: 35g; Fiber: 9g; Sodium: 408mg

CHEESY BROCCOLI SOUP

PREP TIME: 1 hour | **COOK TIME:** 25 minutes | **SERVES:** 4 | Gluten-free, Soy-free

Potatoes are absolutely perfect for creating a thick and creamy texture in soups, stews, and sauces. They are the secret to making this soup oh-so-rich—a little natural fat from the cashews helps, too—and incredibly hearty. The other secret ingredient is the one-two punch of nutritional yeast and lemon juice. It's one of my favorite ways to season without salt and gives the soup its cheesy flavor. This soup is great when made with cauliflower instead of broccoli, too.

½ cup raw cashews

1½ cups hot water

4 Yukon Gold potatoes, unpeeled, diced

½ teaspoon sea salt, or 1 teaspoon Spicy Umami Blend (page 196)

4 cups Vegetable Broth (page 180), **divided**

¼ cup nutritional yeast

3 tablespoons lemon juice

1½ pounds broccoli, stems and florets separated and chopped into bite-size pieces

Freshly ground black pepper (optional)

1. In a bowl, combine the cashews and hot water and soak for 1 hour.

2. In a large saucepan, combine the potatoes, salt, and 3 cups of broth and bring to a boil over medium heat. Lower the heat to medium-low and cook, stirring occasionally, for 10 minutes.

3. Drain and rinse the cashews and transfer them to a blender. Add the remaining 1 cup of broth, the nutritional yeast, and the lemon juice and purée until smooth.

4. Pour the cashew cream into the saucepan, add the broccoli, raise the heat to medium-high, and bring to a boil.

5. Lower the heat to low and simmer for 10 minutes.

6. Serve hot, garnished with pepper, if desired.

PROTEIN BOOST: Add 1 cup cooked or canned white beans for an extra boost of protein.

PER SERVING (1½ CUPS): Calories: 352; Saturated Fat: 2g; Total Fat: 9g; Protein: 15g; Total Carbs: 56g; Fiber: 10g; Sodium: 216mg

YELLOW POTATO SOUP

PREP TIME: 10 minutes | **COOK TIME:** 25 minutes | **SERVES:** 4 | Gluten-free, Nut-free, Soy-free | One-pot

Break out those yellow split peas we used for the Yellow Dal Collard Wraps (page 85), because they are the "cream" and the protein in this healthy, rich potato soup. Why yellow? We eat with our eyes first, so the trick to creating plant-based versions of traditionally nonvegan dishes is to mimic their texture and appearance. I grew up with a very creamy, buttery, yellow potato soup, and here we get that texture and color from plants and spices, not butter.

3 cups cubed potatoes
  (any kind)
1 cup diced onion
1 cup chopped carrots
½ teaspoon chipotle
  chile powder
½ teaspoon ground
  cinnamon
½ teaspoon sea salt, or
  1 teaspoon Spicy Umami
  Blend (page 196)
½ teaspoon ground
  turmeric
¼ teaspoon cayenne pepper
2 cups diced Anjou pear
½ cup dried yellow
  split peas
4 cups Vegetable Broth
  (page 180)
½ teaspoon freshly ground
  black pepper

1. In a large saucepan, combine the potatoes, onion, carrots, chipotle powder, cinnamon, salt, turmeric, and cayenne and dry sauté over medium-high heat for 5 minutes.

2. Add the pear, split peas, and broth and bring to a boil. Lower the heat to medium-low, cover, and simmer until the split peas are tender, 15 to 20 minutes.

3. Serve garnished with the black pepper.

INGREDIENT TIP: You want a very firm pear for this soup, which is why I specifically call for the Anjou variety. Asian pears are fairly firm and work great, too.

PER SERVING (2 CUPS): Calories: 252; Saturated Fat: 0g; Total Fat: 1g; Protein: 9g; Total Carbs: 55g; Fiber: 13g; Sodium: 181mg

GREENS AND GRAINS SOUP

PREP TIME: 5 minutes | **COOK TIME:** 35 minutes | **SERVES:** 6 | Nut-free, Soy-free | One-pot

I enjoy a balanced meal that can be made in one pot and served in one bowl or on one plate. Beans, greens, and grains are at the heart of a healthy plant-based diet, and they're the soul of this soup. Once you get the hang of this recipe, tap into your intuition and begin to play with the combinations, like brown rice, pinto beans, spinach, and some Mexican-style seasonings. The possibilities are nearly endless.

2 cups sliced onions

1 cup diced carrots

1 cup diced celery

1 cup dry farro

1 teaspoon dried basil

1 teaspoon dried oregano

½ teaspoon dried rosemary

½ teaspoon dried thyme

1 (15-ounce) can diced tomatoes

1 (15-ounce) can white kidney beans, drained and rinsed

5 ounces arugula

3 tablespoons lemon juice

1. In a large saucepan, combine the onions, carrots, and celery and dry sauté over medium-high heat, stirring occasionally, until the carrots are softened, about 5 minutes.

2. Add the farro and stir until coated. Add the basil, oregano, rosemary, thyme, and 4 cups water and bring to a boil. Lower the heat to low, cover, and simmer for 30 minutes.

3. Add the tomatoes and beans, raise the heat to medium-high, and bring back to a boil.

4. Add the arugula and lemon juice and cook, stirring, until the arugula is a deep green and lightly wilted, 1 to 2 minutes more.

5. Remove from the heat and serve.

SWAP IT: Wheat berries or pearled barley can be substituted for the farro and cooked for the same amount of time.

PER SERVING (2 CUPS): Calories: 183; Saturated Fat: 0g; Total Fat: 1g; Protein: 9g; Total Carbs: 38g; Fiber: 9g; Sodium: 122mg

HERBY SPLIT PEA SOUP

PREP TIME: 5 minutes | **COOK TIME:** 30 minutes | **SERVES:** 4 | Gluten-free, Nut-free,
Soy-free | One-pot

Let's talk flavor. You may be using some spices you've never heard of in this recipe, like herbes de Provence, and this is a good thing! When cooking healthy dishes without a lot of animal-based fat, spice blends are queen. Italian blends—basil, oregano, and thyme—are pretty common, but this Provençal twist can include fennel, tarragon, and marjoram. I urge you to go to town mixing and matching your favorite dried herbs and spices. Use what you have on hand or what you like—just use 1 tablespoon (3 teaspoons) seasonings total.

¼ cup **Vegetable Broth**
  (page 180)
2 large carrots, diced
2 large celery stalks, diced
1 small russet potato,
  unpeeled, cubed
1 cup dried split peas
1 tablespoon herbes de
  Provence
½ teaspoon sea salt, or
  1½ teaspoons **Spicy
  Umami Blend** (page 196)

1. In a large saucepan, heat the broth over medium-high heat. Add the carrots, celery, and potato and sauté for 5 minutes.

2. Add the split peas, herbes de Provence, and 2 cups water and bring to a boil. Lower the heat to medium-low, cover, and cook for 25 minutes.

3. Stir in the salt and serve.

APPLIANCE TIP: Combine all the ingredients in a multicooker like an Instant Pot or a pressure cooker and cook for 15 minutes on high pressure, then use a quick pressure release.

PER SERVING (1 CUP): Calories: 227; Saturated Fat: 0g; Total Fat: 1g; Protein: 13g; Total Carbs: 43g; Fiber: 15g; Sodium: 205mg

MOROCCAN EGGPLANT STEW

PREP TIME: 5 minutes | **COOK TIME:** 15 minutes | **SERVES:** 4 | Gluten-free, Nut-free, Soy-free | 5-ingredient, One-pot, Quick

Eggplant: Love it or hate it? There was a time when I would only eat it one of two ways: fried or puréed into a smoky baba ghanoush. But I'm a believer in eating the rainbow, and that includes purple—so I decided I would learn to love eggplant. And I did, once I started cooking it Moroccan style. This is delicious over plain brown rice or toasted millet.

2 teaspoons Spicy Umami Blend (page 196)

1 leek, white part only, thinly sliced and rinsed well

1 medium eggplant, diced

2 cups chopped mushrooms

1 tablespoon paprika

2 teaspoons ground cumin

1 teaspoon ground cinnamon

1 (15-ounce) can chickpeas, drained and rinsed

1 (15-ounce) can diced tomatoes

1 cup Vegetable Broth (page 180)

1. In a large saucepan, combine the umami blend and 3 tablespoons water and heat over medium-high heat until bubbling. Add the leek, eggplant, mushrooms, paprika, cumin, and cinnamon and sauté, stirring frequently, for 8 to 10 minutes. If the mixture begins to stick, add water 1 teaspoon at a time as needed.

2. Add the chickpeas, tomatoes, and broth and bring to a boil. Lower the heat to medium-low, cover, and simmer for 10 minutes.

3. Remove from the heat and serve.

SWAP IT: Instead of canned tomatoes, you can use 2 cups chopped fresh tomatoes and add an extra ½ cup vegetable broth.

PER SERVING (2 CUPS): Calories: 200; Saturated Fat: 0g; Total Fat: 3g; Protein: 10g; Total Carbs: 37g; Fiber: 13g; Sodium: 315mg

MINESTRONE IN MINUTES

PREP TIME: 5 minutes | **COOK TIME:** 15 minutes | **SERVES:** 4 to 6 | Gluten-free, Nut-free, Soy-free | One-pot, Quick

Traditional minestrone includes beans and pasta. I've skipped the pasta and doubled the beans to give this soup a one-two protein punch. The result is a thick soup that's great on its own, but wait until you try it ladled over a steaming baked russet or sweet potato or a cup of hearty grains like farro or rice. Yum.

1 cup diced red onion
½ cup diced carrot
½ cup diced celery
2 to 3 garlic cloves, minced
2 teaspoons dried basil
1 (15.5-ounce) can
  cannellini beans, drained
  and rinsed
1 (15.5-ounce) can red
  beans, drained and rinsed
1 (15-ounce) can no-salt
  tomato sauce
3 cups Vegetable Broth
  (page 180)
1 cup diced mushrooms
½ teaspoon red
  pepper flakes
3 tablespoons lemon juice

1. In a large saucepan, heat ¼ cup water over medium-high heat. Add the onion, carrot, celery, and garlic and cook until the vegetables begin to soften, about 3 minutes.

2. Add the basil, cannellini beans, red beans, tomato sauce, broth, mushrooms, and red pepper flakes, stir well, and bring to a boil.

3. Lower the heat to medium-low and cook, stirring occasionally, for about 10 minutes. Remove from the heat and serve.

SWAP IT: Skip the mushrooms and use 1 cup frozen or fresh vegetables. Zucchini, green beans, and peas are all tasty and add a pop of color.

PER SERVING (1½ CUPS): Calories: 267; Saturated Fat: 0g; Total Fat: 1g; Protein: 17g; Total Carbs: 50g; Fiber: 15g; Sodium: 37mg

THREE-BEAN CHILI

PREP TIME: 10 minutes | **COOK TIME:** 25 minutes | **SERVES:** 6 | Gluten-free, Nut-free, Soy-free | One-pot

I keep a wide variety of canned beans and tomatoes in my pantry. If all else fails, I know I can combine them with broth or water and some veggies and end up with a quick soup. Seasoned tomatoes (basil, oregano, and garlic) are especially handy because they eliminate the need to measure spices.

1 cup diced onion

3 teaspoons minced garlic

1 teaspoon chipotle
   chile powder

1 teaspoon paprika

1 teaspoon chili powder

1 teaspoon ground cumin

½ teaspoon red
   pepper flakes

1 (14-ounce) can black
   beans, drained and rinsed

1 (14-ounce) can kidney
   beans, drained and rinsed

1 (14-ounce) can pinto
   beans, drained and rinsed

1 (14.5-ounce) can
   fire-roasted diced
   tomatoes

2 teaspoons tomato paste

3 cups Vegetable Broth
   (page 180)

1 to 2 tablespoons diced
   jalapeño (optional)

½ teaspoon sea salt, or
   1 teaspoon Spicy Umami
   Blend (page 196)

½ teaspoon freshly ground
   black pepper

2 tablespoons lime juice

1. In a large saucepan, heat 2 tablespoons water over medium-high heat. Add the onion and garlic and sauté until the onion is translucent, 5 minutes. Add the chipotle powder, paprika, chili powder, cumin, and red pepper flakes and stir well. Add the black beans, kidney beans, pinto beans, diced tomatoes, tomato paste, broth, jalapeño (if using), salt, and black pepper and bring to a boil.

2. Lower the heat to low, cover, and simmer for 15 minutes.

3. Stir in the lime juice just before serving.

INGREDIENT TIP: Substitute 1½ cups cooked beans for each 14-ounce can.

PAIR IT: Try ladling this chili over some BBQ Baked French Fries (page 161) and drizzle a little Cheesy Chickpea Sauce (page 194) on top.

PER SERVING (2 CUPS): Calories: 220; Saturated Fat: 0g; Total Fat: 2g; Protein: 13g; Total Carbs: 40g; Fiber: 6g; Sodium: 336mg

WHITE CHILI

PREP TIME: 5 minutes | **COOK TIME:** 25 minutes | **SERVES:** 6 | Gluten-free, Nut-free, Soy-free |
One-pot, Quick

I'm always looking for a way to eat more black-eyed peas. Their neutral flavor, creamy texture, and nutrient density—hello, fiber, calcium, and vitamin A—are perfect for so many uses, like whizzed up in a food processor as an alternative to hummus, served with collard greens, or in this white chili.

1 large onion, chopped

4 garlic cloves, minced

2 (4-ounce) cans chopped
green chiles

1 tablespoon ground cumin

1 tablespoon dried oregano

2 teaspoons cayenne pepper

1 (15-ounce) can cannellini
or great Northern beans,
drained and rinsed

1 (15-ounce) can black-eyed
peas, drained and rinsed

4 cups Vegetable Broth
(page 180)

1 teaspoon salt, or
1 tablespoon Spicy Umami
Blend (page 196)

1. In a large saucepan, combine the onion, garlic, green chiles, and ¼ cup water and sauté over medium-high heat until the onion is tender, about 5 minutes.

2. Add the cumin, oregano, cayenne, cannellini beans, black-eyed peas, broth, and salt and bring to a boil.

3. Lower the heat to medium-low, cover, and simmer for 15 minutes. Remove from the heat and serve.

SMART SHOPPING: In love with black-eyed peas? Stock up! Buy several bags of the frozen variety and keep them in your freezer.

PER SERVING (1 CUP): Calories: 138; Saturated Fat: 0g; Total Fat: 1g; Protein: 9g; Total Carbs: 26g; Fiber: 8g; Sodium: 38mg

HOT-AND-SOUR TOFU SOUP

PREP TIME: 5 minutes | **COOK TIME:** 15 minutes | **SERVES:** 2 | Nut-free option | One-pot, Quick

Hello, my name is JL, and I'm a cheater. That's right—I use jarred garlic, frozen diced onions, tomato powder, and, yep, frozen grated ginger. Listen, I use these ingredients often in my cooking, and I'm only human. Sometimes I need some shortcuts. You can find jarred garlic in both the produce section and the condiment aisle in most grocery stores, and Dorot Gardens brand fresh and frozen grated ginger can be found at grocery stores, Walmart, and Target.

¼ cup low-sodium
  soy sauce
2 teaspoons red or yellow
  miso paste
2 teaspoons Red Chili Paste
  (page 191)
1 teaspoon minced garlic
2 teaspoons minced
  fresh ginger
1 cup sliced mushrooms
12 ounces silken tofu
¼ cup crushed peanuts
  (optional)
¼ cup chopped
  green onions

1. In a large saucepan, heat the soy sauce over medium-high heat until it just begins to bubble. Add the miso and whisk and mash it with a fork to create a thick slurry. Add the chili paste, garlic, and ginger and cook, stirring frequently, for 3 minutes.

2. Add the mushrooms and 3 cups water and bring to a boil.

3. Lower the heat to medium-low and add the tofu, crumbling it with your fingers and dropping it into the pan. Cover and simmer for 10 minutes.

4. Divide the crushed peanuts (if using) and green onions between two large bowls. Ladle half the soup into each bowl and serve.

VEGGIE BOOST: Add 1 cup of your favorite frozen veggies (corn, peas, or green beans are nice options) when you crumble in the tofu.

PER SERVING (2 CUPS): Calories: 147; Saturated Fat: 1g; Total Fat: 7g; Protein: 16g; Total Carbs: 9g; Fiber: 2g; Sodium: 1,165mg

SPICY REFRIED BEAN STEW

PREP TIME: 5 minutes | **COOK TIME:** 30 minutes | **SERVES:** 6 | Gluten-free, Nut-free, Soy-free | One-pot

Refried beans are a staple in our house. We make the recipe from my book *Vegan Pressure Cooking* a couple of times a month. They are delicious on salads, as sides, wrapped in collard greens, and, of course, in tacos. And they make this spicy stew oh-so-creamy.

1¼ cups Vegetable Broth (page 180), **divided**

1 small onion, halved and thinly sliced

1 small jalapeño, seeded and finely diced

2 garlic cloves, minced

½ to 1 teaspoon chili powder

½ teaspoon chipotle or ancho chile powder

1 teaspoon Spicy Umami Blend (page 196)

1 (15-ounce) can pinto beans, drained and rinsed

1 (15-ounce) can vegetarian refried beans

1 (14.5-ounce) can no-salt-added diced tomatoes

1. In a large saucepan, heat ¼ cup of broth over medium-high heat. Add the onion, jalapeño, garlic, chili powder, chipotle powder, and umami blend and cook, stirring occasionally, until the onion is tender, about 5 minutes.

2. Add the pinto beans, refried beans, tomatoes, 1 cup water, and remaining 1 cup of broth, stir well, and bring to a boil.

3. Lower the heat to low, cover, and simmer for 20 minutes. Remove from the heat and serve.

PROTEIN BOOST: For a "meaty" chili, swap the canned pinto beans for ½ cup TVP (textured vegetable protein) or 6 ounces extra-firm tofu, crumbled.

INGREDIENT TIP: Use refried pinto or black beans. You can also use 1½ cups cooked pinto beans instead of canned, if you have purchased them frozen or in bulk.

PER SERVING (1½ CUPS): Calories: 150; Saturated Fat: 0g; Total Fat: 1g; Protein: 9g; Total Carbs: 27g; Fiber: 8g; Sodium: 154mg

SWEET POTATO STEW

PREP TIME: 10 minutes | **COOK TIME:** 40 minutes | **SERVES:** 6 | Gluten-free, Nut-free,
Soy-free | One-pot

I've always said that sweet potatoes and black beans are a match made in culinary heaven. Their vibrant colors make them visually appealing, but they're also a dynamic nutrition duo. Black beans are rich in calcium, protein, potassium, and magnesium, and sweet potatoes—a slow carb—are rich in beta-carotene and lower on the glycemic index, meaning they release glucose gradually. And they taste great together.

¼ cup balsamic vinegar

1 large sweet potato, cut into bite-size pieces

1 cup diced onion

½ cup chopped carrot

½ cup chopped celery

2 teaspoons dried thyme

1 teaspoon dried oregano

1 pound Brussels sprouts, halved and thinly sliced

1 (15-ounce) can black beans, drained and rinsed

3 cups Vegetable Broth (page 180)

1 bay leaf

1 teaspoon Spicy Umami Blend (page 196)

½ teaspoon freshly ground black pepper

1. In a large saucepan, heat the vinegar over medium-high heat. Add the sweet potato, onion, carrot, celery, thyme, and oregano and sauté until the sweet potato brightens in color and the onion is tender, about 5 minutes.

2. Add the Brussels sprouts, black beans, broth, bay leaf, umami blend, and pepper, stir well, and bring to a boil.

3. Lower the heat to medium-low and simmer, stirring occasionally, until the sweet potatoes are tender, about 30 minutes. Remove from the heat, discard the bay leaf, and serve.

APPLIANCE TIP: To make this in a multicooker, use the Sauté function for step 1. Add the rest of the ingredients to the pot and cook on low pressure for 8 minutes, then use a natural pressure release.

INGREDIENT TIP: Use 1½ cups cooked black beans instead of canned.

PER SERVING (2 CUPS): Calories: 134; Saturated Fat: 0g; Total Fat: 1g; Protein: 7g; Total Carbs: 27g; Fiber: 8g; Sodium: 49mg

OYSTER (MUSHROOM) STEW

PREP TIME: 10 minutes | **COOK TIME:** 25 minutes | **SERVES:** 2 | Gluten-free option | One-pot

My dad made traditional oyster stew every Christmas Eve. In this plant-based version, I opt for oyster *mushrooms* and a plant-based sauce instead of butter. The creaminess of the sauce comes from beans, plant milk, and some umami-rich miso paste. If you can't find oyster mushrooms, any fresh variety will do here.

¾ cup unsweetened plant-based milk, divided, plus more if needed

1 pound oyster mushrooms, trimmed and cut into thick slices

1 small yellow or sweet onion, diced

3 garlic cloves, minced

2 teaspoons dried sage

1 (15-ounce) can cannellini or great northern beans, drained and rinsed

¼ cup Miso Cream Sauce (page 197)

1 tablespoon low-sodium soy sauce

2 cups Vegetable Broth (page 180), **divided**

2 teaspoons Red Chili Paste (page 191)

1. In a large saucepan, heat ½ cup of plant-based milk over medium-high heat. Add the mushrooms, onion, garlic, and sage and cook until the mushrooms begin to brown, 5 to 8 minutes.

2. Meanwhile, in a blender, combine the beans, miso cream sauce, and remaining ¼ cup of milk and purée until smooth and easy to pour. Add more milk a little at a time, if needed, to reach the desired consistency.

3. Transfer the bean purée to the saucepan and stir well. Add 1 cup of broth and bring to a boil, stirring frequently. Add the remaining 1 cup of broth and stir well. Lower the heat to medium-low, cover, and simmer for 10 minutes.

4. Stir in the chili paste just before serving.

CHANGE IT UP: You can turn this into a cream of mushroom soup easily. Reserve about ½ cup of browned mushrooms. Use an immersion blender to purée the stew directly in the pot (or transfer it to a standing blender), then stir in the reserved browned mushrooms and serve.

ALLERGEN TIP: To make a gluten-free version, be sure to use a nut or seed milk, and replace the soy sauce with tamari that is labeled "gluten-free" or coconut aminos.

PER SERVING (2 CUPS): Calories: 323; Saturated Fat: 1g; Total Fat: 4g; Protein: 23g; Total Carbs: 54g; Fiber: 16g; Sodium: 382mg

NEW ENGLAND CORN CHOWDER

PREP TIME: 5 minutes | **COOK TIME:** 20 minutes | **SERVES:** 6 | Gluten-free, Nut-free option, Soy-free option | Quick

There are a few more steps than usual in this recipe because I wanted to make it extra-special. A mix of chunky and smoother mashed potatoes is the secret to the smooth, thick texture of this plant-based approach to chowder. Aquafaba is the second secret ingredient: I use it to create oil-free roasted corn.

1 pound fingerling potatoes, unpeeled, cut in half

3 tablespoons aquafaba (see Tip, page 178)

1¾ cups fresh, canned, or frozen corn kernels (14 ounces)

1 teaspoon chili powder

1 small sweet onion, diced

2 cups Vegetable Broth (page 180)

2 cups unsweetened plant-based milk, divided

1 teaspoon dried thyme

1 teaspoon dried basil

½ teaspoon freshly ground black pepper

½ teaspoon paprika

1. Place the potatoes in a large saucepan, cover with water, and bring to a boil over medium-high heat. Lower the heat to medium and simmer until the potatoes are tender, 10 to 15 minutes.

2. While the potatoes are cooking, in a large saucepan, heat the aquafaba over medium-high heat. Add the corn and chili powder and cook until the corn begins to brown, about 10 minutes.

3. Drain the potatoes and roughly mash them with a potato masher, leaving some chunks. Set aside.

4. Add the onion, vegetable broth, 1 cup of plant-based milk, the thyme, basil, and pepper to the pan with the corn and bring to a boil.

5. Add the mashed potatoes and remaining 1 cup of milk, stir to combine, and return to a boil. Lower the heat to low and simmer for 5 minutes, then serve.

MAKE IT FASTER: Opt for fire-roasted frozen corn, omit the aquafaba and chili powder, and skip step 2.

PER SERVING (1½ CUPS): Calories: 187; Saturated Fat: 0g; Total Fat: 2g; Protein: 7g; Total Carbs: 38g; Fiber: 5g; Sodium: 67mg

MUSHROOM AND QUINOA "GUMBO"

PREP TIME: 15 to 30 minutes | **COOK TIME:** 30 minutes | **SERVES:** 6 | Gluten-free, Nut-free,
Soy-free | One-pot

Gumbo usually stars meat or shellfish and it all begins with a fat-and-flour-based roux. In this version, I've skipped the animal protein and returned to the traditional gumbo thickener: filé powder, or ground sassafras leaves. This inexpensive spice is a dream. It helps create the dark brown, nearly gravy-like sauce that I look for when making gumbo. And you can bet I'm starting with the Cajun version of mirepoix (see page 49), known as the Holy Trinity: chopped onion, bell pepper, and celery.

2 cups chopped portobello
  mushrooms
¼ cup balsamic vinegar
1 cup chopped onion
1 cup chopped green
  bell pepper
1 cup chopped celery
1 tablespoon filé powder
1 tablespoon tomato
  powder, or 2 teaspoons
  tomato paste
1 teaspoon dried basil
1 teaspoon cayenne pepper
1 teaspoon dried thyme
3 cups Vegetable Broth
  (page 180), **divided**
½ cup dry quinoa, rinsed
  and drained
4 cups chopped
  mustard greens

1. In a large skillet, combine the mushrooms and vinegar. Set aside to marinate for 15 to 30 minutes.

2. Place the skillet over medium-high heat and cook the mushrooms for 3 minutes. Add the onion, bell pepper, and celery and cook for 3 minutes more. Add the filé, stir to coat the vegetables, and cook, stirring frequently, for 5 minutes more.

3. Add the tomato powder, basil, cayenne, thyme, 2 cups of broth, and the quinoa and bring to a boil.

4. Lower the heat to medium-low, cover, and cook until the quinoa is tender, about 15 minutes.

5. Raise the heat to medium-high, add the mustard greens and remaining 1 cup of broth, stir to combine, and bring the mixture back to a boil.

6. Lower the heat to low, cover, and simmer for 5 minutes more. Remove from the heat and serve.

INGREDIENT TIP: Filé powder is a fantastic salt-free spice that you can use in all kinds of recipes, stews, soup, and sauces. It thickens *and* creates a slightly sweet contrast in savory dishes.

SWAP IT: Use arugula or spinach instead of mustard greens.

PER SERVING (2 CUPS): Calories: 97; Saturated Fat: 0g; Total Fat: 1g; Protein: 4g; Total Carbs: 18g; Fiber: 4g; Sodium: 29mg

CHAPTER 7

MAIN ATTRACTIONS

THE HIPPIE BOWL FORMULA

PREP TIME: 10 to 15 minutes | **COOK TIME:** 20 to 45 minutes | **SERVES:** 2 | Gluten-free option, Nut-free option, Soy-free

This very simple formula kicks off the Main Attractions chapter because I want you to know how simple it is to create a plant-based meal. I've intentionally left out specific amounts for the variation ingredients because I want to give you some independence. But for general guidance on cooking grains, see page 24.

THE FORMULA

1½ cups cooked grains or
   roasted potatoes
1 (15-ounce) can beans, drained
   and rinsed, or 1½ cups
   cooked beans
4 to 5 cups cooked or raw
   vegetables

SPICY BOWL

Cooked brown rice
Pinto beans simmered
  in vegetable broth
  with ground cumin and
  chili powder
Steamed kale tossed with
  lime juice

CURRY BOWL

Roasted Yukon Gold potatoes
Chickpeas or lentils
  simmered in coconut
  milk with spinach, ground
  turmeric, curry powder, and
  ground ginger

LITTLE ITALY BOWL

Cooked farro
Cannellini beans and diced
  tomatoes simmered with
  arugula, capers, dried
  oregano, dried basil, and
  dried parsley

Spoon the cooked grains or roasted potatoes into bowls. Top with the cooked beans and veggies.

MAKE AHEAD: This is the *perfect* way to use batch-cooked grains, potatoes, and beans. Prep over the weekend, then reheat and eat during the week.

PER SERVING (2 CUPS): Calories: 594; Saturated Fat: 1g; Total Fat: 4g; Protein: 28g; Total Carbs: 113g; Fiber: 34g; Sodium: 137mg

UMAMI OAT BURGERS

PREP TIME: 10 minutes | **COOK TIME:** 50 minutes | **MAKES:** 8 | Gluten-free, Nut-free, Soy-free

A simple and flavorful veggie burger is a must in your plant-based cooking arsenal. This one is great to serve on bread or a bun or even wrapped up in a collard leaf. But you can also crumble a patty and serve it over a salad or stir it into soup or chili for a little oomph. The burger already has three of the vegan food groups—beans, grains, and seeds—so all you need to do is add a handful or two of arugula to the mixture before mashing to have the ultimate well-rounded meal.

1 pound sweet potatoes, unpeeled, cut into 1-inch chunks

1 teaspoon smoked paprika, divided

½ teaspoon garlic powder

½ teaspoon ground cumin

1 (15-ounce) can kidney or red beans, drained and rinsed, or 1½ cups cooked beans (see page 24)

1 cup gluten-free rolled oats

½ cup chopped green onions

1 tablespoon Smoky Ketchup (page 193)

2 teaspoons Spicy Umami Blend (page 196)

1 teaspoon black sesame seeds

¼ teaspoon ground mustard

Vegetable oil spray (optional)

1. Preheat the oven to 400°F. Line a baking sheet with parchment paper or a silicone baking mat.

2. In a medium bowl, toss together the sweet potatoes, ½ teaspoon of paprika, the garlic powder, and the cumin until evenly coated.

3. Spread the potatoes in a single layer on the prepared baking sheet and bake for 30 to 35 minutes, until tender.

4. In a large bowl, combine the sweet potatoes, beans, oats, green onions, smoky ketchup, umami blend, sesame seeds, ground mustard, and remaining ½ teaspoon paprika. Using your hands or a potato masher, mash everything together (or combine the ingredients in a food processor and pulse until combined).

5. Form the mixture into 8 patties.

6. Spray a large skillet with vegetable oil (or use a nonstick skillet). Cook the patties over medium-high heat for 6 minutes, then flip and cook for about 6 minutes more.

APPLIANCE TIP: For my air-frying friends, you can speed the process up immensely while getting a great texture with no spray oil. In step 3, air-fry at 370°F for 18 minutes. In step 6, air-fry at 390°F for 5 minutes, flip the patties, and air-fry for 5 minutes more.

INGREDIENT TIP: Use 1½ cups cooked beans instead of canned.

PER SERVING (1 PATTY): Calories: 129; Saturated Fat: 0g; Total Fat: 1g; Protein: 6g; Total Carbs: 25g; Fiber: 5g; Sodium: 6mg

BAKED CHICKPEA CUTLETS AND MASHED POTATOES

PREP TIME: 15 minutes | **COOK TIME:** 30 minutes | **MAKES:** 4 cutlets | Gluten-free option, Soy-free option

Hey, remember the Veggie Lunch Muffins (page 91)? These cutlets are a variation of those muffins, because I'm a firm believer in repurposing recipes so you can opt for autopilot cooking yet still get a variety of textures and flavor profiles. I've switched up the beans and opted for a different cooking method, resulting in an entirely different meal.

1½ pounds Yukon gold or creamer potatoes, unpeeled, quartered

1 tablespoon ground flaxseed

3 tablespoons warm water

1 (15-ounce) can chickpeas, drained (liquid reserved) and rinsed

½ cup unsweetened coconut milk

¼ cup plus 1 tablespoon nutritional yeast, divided

1 cup grated yellow squash

1 cup finely chopped red bell pepper

1 cup chopped fresh spinach

2 teaspoons Spicy Umami Blend (page 196), or 1 teaspoon sea salt

½ cup whole-wheat flour

½ cup bread crumbs or crumbled cornflakes

1. Preheat the oven to 375°F. Line a baking sheet with parchment paper or a silicone baking mat.

2. Fill a large saucepan with water and bring to a boil over high heat. Add the potatoes and cook until tender, 15 to 20 minutes.

3. Meanwhile, in a small bowl or measuring cup, whisk together the ground flaxseed and warm water. Set aside.

4. In a food processor, combine the chickpeas, coconut milk, and 1 tablespoon of nutritional yeast and process until smooth and creamy. Transfer the mixture to a large bowl.

5. Add the flaxseed mixture, squash, bell pepper, spinach, and umami blend to the chickpea mixture and stir until combined. Form the mixture into 4 cutlets. Set aside.

6. Pour 3 tablespoons aquafaba into a wide, shallow bowl.

7. On a large plate, mix together the flour, bread crumbs, and arrowroot.

1 teaspoon arrowroot
  powder or potato starch
3 tablespoons lemon juice
1 tablespoon plus
  4 teaspoons Plant Butter
  (page 179), **divided**
½ teaspoon freshly ground
  black or white pepper

8. Dip each cutlet in the aquafaba and then place on the plate with the coating mixture. Using your fingers, sprinkle the coating over the top of each cutlet. Gently turn over the cutlets while pressing the coating against them to adhere. Transfer the cutlets to the prepared baking sheet and bake for 15 minutes.

9. Drain the potatoes and return them to the pan. Add the lemon juice, remaining ¼ cup of nutritional yeast, 1 tablespoon of butter, and pepper and mash with a potato masher.

10. Place the cutlets onto individual serving plates and top each with 1 to 1½ cups of the mashed potatoes and the remaining 1 teaspoon of butter.

ALLERGEN TIPS: For gluten-free cutlets, opt for crushed cornflakes instead of bread crumbs and use chickpea flour instead of wheat flour. For soy-free cutlets, use a non-soy unsweetened plant-based milk instead of Plant Butter for mashing.

PER SERVING (1 CUTLET): Calories: 456; Saturated Fat: 7g; Total Fat: 16g; Protein: 15g; Total Carbs: 69g; Fiber: 11g; Sodium: 435mg

BLACK-EYED PEA AND SWEET POTATO CASSEROLE

PREP TIME: 10 minutes | **COOK TIME:** 35 minutes | **MAKES:** 9 pieces | Gluten-free option, Nut-free, Soy-free option

A nod to shepherd's pie, this twist is a casserole with just a few wholesome main ingredients and lots of flavorful spices.

1 pound sweet potatoes or yams, unpeeled, cubed

¼ cup Vegetable Broth (page 180)

½ cup diced onion

2 garlic cloves, minced

1 pound collard greens, leaves stemmed and shredded

1 (15-ounce) can black-eyed peas, drained and rinsed

1 cup unsweetened plant-based milk, divided

1 tablespoon low-sodium soy sauce

½ teaspoon cayenne pepper

½ teaspoon chili powder

½ teaspoon chipotle chile powder

¼ teaspoon freshly ground black pepper

1. Preheat the oven to 400°F. Line an 8-inch square baking pan with parchment paper (or use a non-stick pan).

2. Place the potatoes in a large saucepan, cover with water, and bring to a boil over medium-high heat. Lower the heat to medium and cook until the potatoes are tender, 10 to 15 minutes.

3. In a large skillet, heat the broth over medium-high heat. Add the onion, garlic, and collard greens and cook until the collards turn bright green and the onion softens, 3 to 5 minutes.

4. Add the black-eyed peas, ¾ cup of plant-based milk, the soy sauce, cayenne, chili powder, and chipotle powder and stir to combine. Bring to a boil, then remove from the heat and transfer the mixture to the prepared baking pan.

5. Drain the potatoes and return them to the saucepan. Add the remaining ¼ cup of milk and mash with a potato masher. Spread the mashed potatoes over the black-eyed pea mixture in the baking pan and sprinkle with the black pepper.

6. Bake for 25 minutes, until the potatoes are firm and slightly crusty.

INGREDIENT TIP: If using home-cooked black-eyed peas, use about 2 cups. A thawed 12-ounce bag of frozen black-eyed peas works great, too.

ALLERGEN TIP: To make this gluten-free and soy-free, use coconut aminos instead of soy sauce and a plant milk other than soy milk.

PER SERVING (1 PIECE): Calories: 119; Saturated Fat: 0g; Total Fat: 1g; Protein: 6g; Total Carbs: 23g; Fiber: 7g; Sodium: 127mg

TOFU "RIBS"

PREP TIME: 1 hour | **COOK TIME:** 20 minutes | **MAKES:** 10 pieces | Gluten-free, Nut-free

This is one of those omni-pleasing recipes. Listen, I'm not trying to fool anyone here—that's never my plan. Instead, I try to evoke flavor and texture memories that make a plant-based version of an old favorite satisfying to eat. The stringy jackfruit, combined with firm tofu and then smothered in sauce, creates a juicy, meaty bite. Serve this up with Cauliflower Florets 'n' "Cheese" (page 136) for a good ol' plant-based barbecue.

1 (14-ounce) block
  extra-firm tofu, pressed
  (see page 23) **and drained**
1 (14-ounce) can
  jackfruit, drained
1 cup chopped mushrooms
  (any kind)
¼ cup nutritional yeast
2 tablespoons ground
  flaxseed
½ cup BBQ Sauce (page 189)

1. Preheat the oven to 375°F. Line an 8-inch square baking pan with parchment paper.

2. In a food processor, combine the tofu, jackfruit, and mushrooms and pulse to chop and form a chunky texture. Transfer the mixture to a medium bowl. Add the nutritional yeast and ground flaxseed and stir to combine.

3. Spread ¼ cup of BBQ sauce over the bottom of the prepared baking pan. Transfer the tofu mixture to the pan and spread it out evenly with a spatula. Pour the remaining ¼ cup of BBQ sauce over the top and spread it evenly to cover the tofu mixture.

4. Bake for 30 minutes. Transfer the pan to a wire rack and let cool for 30 minutes.

5. Cut into 10 "ribs" and serve.

INGREDIENT TIP: Are you in love with jackfruit? You can purchase it in bulk in large bags. Once opened, however, you need to use it within 4 to 5 days. Plan a jackfruit cooking day and make several recipes at once, and you'll save a little money!

PER SERVING (2 PIECES): Calories: 227; Saturated Fat: 1g; Total Fat: 6g; Protein: 12g; Total Carbs: 35g; Fiber: 2g; Sodium: 76mg

BLACK BEAN CAULIFLOWER STEAKS

PREP TIME: 15 minutes | **COOK TIME:** 20 minutes | **SERVES:** 2 | Gluten-free, Nut-free, Soy-free

I love cauliflower steak as a meal *if* it's paired appropriately with a hearty schmear of protein. Serve this version at a dinner party, and you'll feel like a culinary rock star. It's easy to prepare, beautiful to serve, and delicious to eat.

1 large head cauliflower

¼ cup plus 1 tablespoon balsamic vinegar, divided

2 teaspoons Spicy Umami Blend (page 196), **or** 1 teaspoon salt, divided

1 (15-ounce) can black beans, drained and rinsed, or 1½ cups cooked black beans

4 ounces sun-dried tomatoes (see Tip)

¼ cup chopped fresh cilantro (optional)

1. Preheat the oven to 400°F. Line a baking sheet with parchment paper or a silicone baking mat.

2. Remove the outer green leaves from the head of cauliflower but do not remove the stem. Cut the cauliflower in half through the stem. From each half, gently cut two 1-inch-thick steaks for a total of 4 steaks. Place the steaks on the prepared baking sheet.

3. Pour ¼ cup of vinegar over the steaks and sprinkle with 1 teaspoon of umami blend. Bake for 10 minutes, then flip each steak and sprinkle the remaining 1 teaspoon of umami blend over the tops. Bake for 10 minutes more.

4. While the cauliflower is baking, in a food processor, combine the black beans, sun-dried tomatoes, and remaining 1 tablespoon of vinegar and purée until smooth and creamy.

5. To serve, spread ¼ cup of black bean purée on a salad plate. Place one steak on top, add a ¼-cup dollop of the purée, top with a second steak, and scoop another ¼ cup of the purée on top. Garnish with 2 tablespoons of cilantro. Repeat for the second serving.

INGREDIENT TIP: If using dry sun-dried tomatoes, soak them in boiling water for 10 minutes before using them.

PER SERVING (2 STEAKS AND ¾ CUP PURÉE): Calories: 450; Saturated Fat: 1g; Total Fat: 4g; Protein: 28g; Total Carbs: 88g; Fiber: 27g; Sodium: 756mg

SCALLOPED HEARTS OF PALM PROVENÇAL

PREP TIME: 10 minutes | **COOK TIME:** 25 minutes | **SERVES:** 2 | Gluten-free, Nut-free, Soy-free | One-pot

One of the fun things about cooking plant-based is getting creative and finding ways to make versions of pre-vegan favorites. I've discovered that hearts of palm and artichoke hearts are two vegetables that stand in beautifully for seafood. And if you cut hearts of palm into thick slices, it's a perfect replacement for scallops and contributes umami-rich flavor from the brine and a similar tender texture.

1 (14-ounce) can or jar
  hearts of palm, drained
¼ cup balsamic vinegar
2 tablespoons
  minced shallot
3 garlic cloves, minced
1 large tomato, chopped
1 (15-ounce) can small red
  beans, drained and rinsed,
  or 1½ cups cooked small
  red beans
½ cup red wine or red
  wine vinegar
Fresh parsley, for garnish
  (optional)

1. Cut the hearts of palm into ½-inch-thick rounds. Place them on a tea towel or paper towel and pat dry.

2. In a large nonstick skillet, sear the hearts of palm over high heat until browned, 2 to 4 minutes on each side. Set aside.

3. In the same skillet, combine the vinegar, shallot, and garlic and sauté over medium-high heat until the shallot is tender, about 3 minutes. Add the tomato, beans, and wine and cook, stirring occasionally, until the mixture begins to gently bubble, about 8 minutes.

4. Lower the heat to low, gently nestle the hearts of palm into the mixture, cover, and simmer for 5 minutes. Remove from the heat and garnish with fresh parsley, if using. Serve.

INGREDIENT TIP: Small red beans are mild and creamy and can be found canned and dried. Pinto, kidney, or adzuki beans can also be used in this recipe.

PER SERVING (2 CUPS): Calories: 464; Saturated Fat: 0g; Total Fat: 2g; Protein: 18g; Total Carbs: 91g; Fiber: 4g; Sodium: 403mg

SUMMER SQUASH LASAGNA

PREP TIME: 10 minutes | **COOK TIME:** 25 minutes | **SERVES:** 4 | Gluten-free, Nut-free, Soy-free

Zucchini seems to be the low-carb darling of choice for those trying to replace traditional pasta noodles in Italian-style recipes. But its yellow cousin, summer squash, is a great fill-in! Here, the squash serves as a casserole-type base, and the creamy bean purée makes this dish wholesome yet comforting.

Vegetable oil spray
(optional)

2 (15-ounce) cans cannellini beans, drained and rinsed, or 3 cups cooked cannellini beans

½ cup nutritional yeast

2 tablespoons red wine vinegar or balsamic vinegar

2 teaspoons dried basil

1 teaspoon garlic powder

2 cups "Meaty" Marinara (page 187), **divided**

2 yellow squash, cut into ¼-inch-thick slices

1 teaspoon freshly ground black pepper

½ teaspoon Spicy Umami Blend (page 196), or ¼ teaspoon salt

1. Preheat the oven to 375°F. Spray an 8-inch square baking pan with vegetable oil (or use a nonstick baking pan).

2. In a food processor or blender, combine the cannellini beans, nutritional yeast, vinegar, basil, and garlic powder and pulse until the mixture has a creamy, cottage cheese–like consistency.

3. Spread ¼ cup of marinara over the bottom of the prepared baking pan. Place squash rounds in a single layer over the marinara. Pour ¼ cup of marinara over the squash. Dollop about ½ cup of the bean mixture over the marinara. Add another layer of squash, ½ cup of sauce, and ½ cup of bean mixture. Repeat the layers one more time. Pour the remaining sauce over the top and dot with the remaining bean mixture. Sprinkle with the pepper and umami blend.

4. Bake for 15 minutes, or until the sauce is bubbling and the bean mixture browns.

5. Transfer to a wire rack and let sit for 10 minutes, then slice into 8 pieces and serve.

SWAP IT: To make this cheesier, use only one 15-ounce can of beans and add one 8-ounce container Kite Hill ricotta (made from cultured almond milk).

PER SERVING (2 PIECES): Calories: 291; Saturated Fat: 0g; Total Fat: 3g; Protein: 20g; Total Carbs: 50g; Fiber: 16g; Sodium: 169mg

ZOODLE SPAGHETTI MARINARA

PREP TIME: 10 minutes | **COOK TIME:** 10 minutes | **SERVES:** 4 | Gluten-free, Nut-free, Soy-free | Quick

Well, *of course* I still want to use zoodles, because zucchini noodles are a low-carb alternative to pasta and they're so much fun to make! You'll be using four—FOUR— zucchini, one per person. I have you topping them off with marinara sauce, but if you're cooking for just two, set aside two portions of the zoodles to use as a simple side for Umami Oat Burgers (page 120) or as a base for Quinoa Pilaf (page 138).

2 tablespoons Vegetable
  Broth (page 180)

1 teaspoon minced garlic

4 medium zucchini,
  spiralized

½ teaspoon dried basil

½ teaspoon dried oregano

¼ to ½ teaspoon red
  pepper flakes

¼ teaspoon salt (optional)

¼ teaspoon freshly ground
  black pepper

2 cups "Meaty" Marinara
  (page 187)

1. In a large skillet, heat the broth over medium-high heat. Add the garlic, zucchini, basil, oregano, red pepper flakes, salt (if using), and black pepper and sauté until the zucchini is barely tender, 1 to 2 minutes.

2. Divide the zoodles evenly among four bowls. Spoon ½ cup of hot marinara sauce over each bowl and serve.

PROTEIN BOOST: Add crumbled tempeh, tofu, or seitan to the marinara sauce to make it even "meatier."

PER SERVING (1 CUP): Calories: 102; Saturated Fat: 0g; Total Fat: 3g; Protein: 5g; Total Carbs: 16g; Fiber: 5g; Sodium: 178mg

BUFFALO CAULIFLOWER PIZZA

PREP TIME: 15 minutes | **COOK TIME:** 25 minutes | **MAKES:** 2 individual pizzas | Gluten-free, Nut-free, Soy-free option

Do you have neglected pie pans in your cupboard? Get 'em out! This is a fun way to make an uber-healthy "pizza."

1 head cauliflower
1 flax egg (see page 178)
½ cup chickpea flour
¼ cup nutritional yeast
1 cup Buffalo Sauce
  (page 190; use non-soy
  vegan butter if soy-free)
1 cup diced onion
2 cups chopped mushrooms
8 fresh basil leaves

1. Preheat the oven to 400°F. Line two 8- or 9-inch pie pans with parchment paper.

2. Remove the leaves from the head of cauliflower, tear off the florets, and discard the stem. Transfer the florets to a food processor and pulse until the cauliflower is broken down into pieces the size of grains of rice.

3. Transfer the riced cauliflower to a medium bowl. Add the flax egg, chickpea flour, and nutritional yeast and stir to combine. Place half the mixture into each prepared pie pan. Using your fingers, press the mixture over the bottoms of the pans, spreading it out to about ⅓ inch thick (it doesn't have to completely cover the pans).

4. Bake for 15 minutes. Transfer the pie pans to a wire rack; keep the oven on.

5. To assemble the pizzas, pour ½ cup of Buffalo sauce over the top of one crust and spread it out evenly to cover. Sprinkle ½ cup of onion and 1 cup of mushrooms over the top. Repeat with the second crust.

6. Place the pizzas back in the oven and bake for 10 minutes.

7. Garnish each pizza with 4 basil leaves and serve.

INGREDIENT TIP: Frozen cauliflower also works for this crust. Thaw and drain it, then use a tea towel to wring out excess liquid.

PER SERVING (1 PIZZA): Calories: 498; Saturated Fat: 4g; Total Fat: 35g; Protein: 18g; Total Carbs: 43g; Fiber: 11g; Sodium: 584mg

SHOYU RAMEN

PREP TIME: 15 minutes | **COOK TIME:** 30 minutes | **SERVES:** 4 | Gluten-free option,
Nut-free option | One-pot

You probably know ramen noodles as the cheap package of dry noodles with a super-salty spice mix. But go to your favorite Asian market or browse the international aisle of your local grocer and you'll see ramen noodles—sans spice mix—right next to the soba and rice noodles. Hakubaku brand is organic, and Lotus Foods makes a gluten-free ramen noodle with brown rice and millet.

¼ cup low-sodium soy sauce or tamari

2 teaspoons Spicy Umami Blend (page 196)

1 (2-inch) piece fresh ginger, peeled and grated

4 garlic cloves, minced

4 cups Vegetable Broth (page 180)

2 cups chopped shiitake mushrooms

1 cup shredded carrots

6 ounces dry ramen noodles

4 cups fresh baby spinach

½ cup chopped green onions

1 tablespoon Red Chili Paste (page 191), **for garnish**

4 tablespoons chopped peanuts, for garnish (optional)

1. In a large saucepan, combine the soy sauce, umami blend, ginger, and garlic and sauté over medium-high heat until aromatic, 3 to 5 minutes. Add the broth and 2 cups water and bring to a boil. Lower the heat to medium-low, add the mushrooms and carrots, and simmer for 10 minutes.

2. Raise the heat to medium-high, add the noodles, and cook for 4 minutes more.

3. Remove from the heat and stir in the spinach and green onions.

4. Serve each bowl garnished with a dollop of chili paste and 1 tablespoon of peanuts, if desired.

SWAP IT: About 1 ounce dried mushrooms can be used in place of fresh. They will make the broth even earthier.

ALLERGEN TIP: To make this gluten-free, use tamari labeled "gluten-free" and replace the ramen noodles with rice noodles.

PER SERVING (1½ CUPS): Calories: 206; Saturated Fat: 0g; Total Fat: 0g; Protein: 9g; Total Carbs: 42g; Fiber: 4g; Sodium: 1232mg

VEGGIE PHO

PREP TIME: 15 minutes | **COOK TIME:** 40 minutes | **SERVES:** 2 | Gluten-free option, Nut-free, Soy-free option

This quick pho has lots of flavor. If you'd rather not invest in whole jars of cloves and star anise, look for a local grocer that sells spices in bulk and just buy what you need.

4 cups Vegetable Broth
(page 180)
1 (2-inch) piece fresh
ginger, peeled and
thinly sliced
2 tablespoons low-sodium
soy sauce or tamari
2 whole cloves
2 star anise pods
1 cinnamon stick
1 (14-ounce) block firm or
extra-firm tofu, pressed
(see page 23) and drained
2 tablespoons rice vinegar
2 jalapeños, seeded and
thinly sliced
1 small onion, halved and
thinly sliced
1 large carrot, diced
8 ounces dry rice noodles
1 cup chopped fresh basil
½ cup chopped fresh
cilantro
2 teaspoons Red Chili Paste
(page 191)

1. In a large saucepan, combine the broth, ginger, soy sauce, cloves, star anise, and cinnamon stick and bring to a boil over medium-high heat. Lower the heat to medium-low and simmer for 30 minutes.

2. Cut the tofu into 16 cubes. Set aside.

3. In a skillet, bring the vinegar to a boil over medium-high heat. Add the jalapeños, onion, and carrot and sauté for 3 minutes. Add the tofu and cook, stirring gently, for 10 minutes.

4. In a large saucepan, bring 4 cups water to a boil over high heat. Add the rice noodles and cook for only 1 minute. Drain, rinse well, and drain again. Set aside.

5. After the broth has finished simmering, use a slotted spoon to remove the cloves, star anise, and cinnamon stick.

6. Divide the noodles between two bowls. Top each with half the tofu mixture and half the basil. Pour 2 cups of broth into each bowl. Top each with half the cilantro and half the chili paste and serve.

ALLERGEN TIP: To make this gluten-free, use a tamari that is labeled "gluten-free." For a soy-free version, use coconut aminos instead of soy sauce and replace the tofu with mushrooms.

PER SERVING (3 CUPS): Calories: 642; Saturated Fat: 1g; Total Fat: 13g; Protein: 29g; Total Carbs: 104g; Fiber: 5g; Sodium: 664mg

CAULIFLOWER FLORETS 'N' "CHEESE"

PREP TIME: 10 minutes │ **COOK TIME:** 10 minutes │ **SERVES:** 2 │ Gluten-free, Nut-free, Soy-free option │ One-pot, Quick

This is *such* a fun play on mac 'n' cheese! Cauliflower stands in for pasta and the cheesy sauce gives it some zing. Great as a side dish, when you add some diced baked tofu or tempeh it becomes a hearty entrée. Bonus: Try this with broccoli or . . . wait for it . . . Brussels sprouts!

1 head cauliflower, cut
　into florets
3 tablespoons lemon juice
1½ cups Cheesy Chickpea
　Sauce (page 194)
½ teaspoon freshly ground
　black pepper
1 teaspoon smoked paprika
¼ cup chopped
　green onions

1. Fill a large saucepan with about 2 inches of water, insert a steamer basket, and bring to a boil over high heat. Lower the heat to medium-high and place the cauliflower in the steamer. Cover and steam until the cauliflower is fork-tender, 5 to 7 minutes.

2. Remove the steamer and pour the water out of the saucepan. Transfer the cauliflower to the saucepan and place over medium heat. Add the lemon juice and cheesy sauce and stir gently, until the cauliflower is evenly coated. Cook, stirring, until the sauce just begins to bubble.

3. Spoon the mixture into two bowls, sprinkle each with ½ teaspoon of paprika and 2 tablespoons of green onion, then serve.

SWAP IT: No cheesy sauce? In a bowl, mix together the 3 tablespoons lemon juice called for in the recipe, 1/4 cup nutritional yeast, and 1 cup unsweetened plant-based milk and add it instead of the cheesy sauce in step 2.

PER SERVING (2 CUPS): Calories: 304; Saturated Fat: 0g; Total Fat: 4g; Protein: 18g; Total Carbs: 53g; Fiber: 16g; Sodium: 671mg

LOADED GREEN CURRY

PREP TIME: 10 minutes | **COOK TIME:** 15 minutes | **SERVES:** 4 | Gluten-free, Soy-free | One-pot, Quick

Curry is so misunderstood. Many avoid it because they think it's too hot. But curry is a leaf and, once ground, is combined with a variety of spices. Yes, some curries are spicy, but others aren't at all. Many fiery curry bowls are made with mild curry and are spicy because they include lots of chiles. My point? This green curry is mild, flavorful, and veggie-filled. Try it.

1 large tomato, diced

3 to 4 garlic cloves, minced

2 teaspoons curry powder

1 (1-inch) piece fresh ginger, peeled and grated

1 teaspoon ground mustard

1 teaspoon ground turmeric

1 head broccoli, crown cut into florets, stem peeled and diced

1 (10-ounce) package frozen green peas, or 1½ cups canned or fresh peas

1 (13.5-ounce) can coconut milk

8 ounces fresh baby spinach

½ cup chopped green onions

¼ cup crushed peanuts (optional)

1. In a large skillet, combine the tomatoes, garlic, curry powder, ginger, ground mustard, and turmeric and sauté over medium-high heat for 5 minutes. Add the broccoli and cook, without stirring, for 5 minutes. Add the peas and coconut milk, stir to combine, and bring to a boil.

2. Lower the heat to low, stir in the spinach, cover, and simmer for 10 minutes.

3. Serve garnished with the green onions and crushed peanuts, if desired.

INGREDIENT TIP: Okay, spice lovers, you *can* kick this up if you want! Add jalapeño or bhut jolokia (ghost pepper) powder. Start with a teaspoon and go from there.

PER SERVING (1½ CUPS): Calories: 308; Saturated Fat: 18g; Total Fat: 22g; Protein: 11g; Total Carbs: 25g; Fiber: 8g; Sodium: 168mg

QUINOA PILAF

PREP TIME: 10 minutes | **COOK TIME:** 20 minutes | **SERVES:** 4 | Gluten-free, Soy-free | One-pot, Quick

There's no easier way to make an everyday grain special than to add vegetables (that's my mantra). Seriously, when you're bulk cooking on the weekend and thinking, "No more brown rice," add some veggies and see how that changes your opinion. In this case, by adding onion and carrots to quinoa—an honorary legume—I've turned a "side" into a hearty entrée.

½ cup chopped red onion

1 cup diced carrots

½ teaspoon dried parsley

½ teaspoon dried thyme

1 cup dry quinoa, rinsed
   and drained

1½ cups Vegetable Broth
   (page 180)

¼ cup chopped walnuts

Chopped fresh parsley or
   thyme, for garnish

1. In a large saucepan, dry sauté the onion and carrots over medium-high heat, stirring frequently to prevent sticking, until the onion is tender, 3 to 5 minutes. Add the parsley, thyme, quinoa, and broth and bring to a boil.

2. Lower the heat to medium-low, cover, and cook for 15 minutes.

3. Remove the pan from the heat and let sit for 5 minutes.

4. Fluff the quinoa with a fork, add the walnuts, and gently mix until combined.

5. Spoon into bowls and serve garnished with fresh parsley.

CHANGE IT UP: If you like to cook plain grains in bulk—think rice, farro, and millet—you can transform them by sautéing onion and carrot in a skillet as directed above, adding 1 or 2 cups cooked grains (no vegetable broth), and stir-frying until hot.

PER SERVING (1½ CUPS): Calories: 230; Saturated Fat: 1g; Total Fat: 7g; Protein: 8g; Total Carbs: 34g; Fiber: 5g; Sodium: 37mg

CREAMY EDAMAME BULGUR BOWL

PREP TIME: 20 minutes | **COOK TIME:** 20 minutes | **SERVES:** 4 | 5-ingredient, Quick

Bulgur is a common Middle Eastern ingredient. The groats are filled with fiber and pack some protein, too. This fluffy grain adds texture while keeping the overall mouthfeel of a dish light and airy. An equal costar in this simple bowl, edamame provides a textural contrast. You could easily serve this bowl with peanut sauce or a dressing of your choice, but I strongly encourage you try it with the Miso Cream Sauce.

1 cup medium-grind bulgur

10 ounces frozen shelled edamame, thawed

1 red bell pepper, seeded and diced

1 cup Miso Cream Sauce (page 197)

1. In a saucepan, combine the bulgur and 1½ cups water and bring to a boil over medium-high heat. Lower the heat to medium-low, cover, and cook until tender, about 12 minutes. Remove the saucepan from the heat and let stand, covered, for 10 minutes.

2. In a large bowl, combine the edamame and bell pepper. Set aside.

3. Fluff the bulgur with a fork and transfer it to the bowl with the vegetables. Gently fold until combined.

4. Spoon into four bowls, drizzle ¼ cup of miso cream sauce over each serving, and serve.

MAKE AHEAD: To make this in advance, stir the Miso Cream Sauce directly into the bowl, transfer to an airtight container, and refrigerate for up to 4 days. Serve as a cold salad.

PER SERVING (2 CUPS): Calories: 346; Saturated Fat: 2g; Total Fat: 11g; Protein: 18g; Total Carbs: 46g; Fiber: 10g; Sodium: 388mg

PINTO PAELLA

PREP TIME: 10 minutes | **COOK TIME:** 30 to 35 minutes | **MAKES:** 4 | Gluten-free, Nut-free, Soy-free | One-pot

Once again, I'm taking some liberties with tradition. This paella is meat-free—obviously—but I am also bringing in pinto beans to "beef" it up, so to speak. I love using corn with pinto beans, but you can use any kind of frozen vegetable you prefer.

¼ cup red wine vinegar

4 garlic cloves, minced

1 large red onion, diced

1 large red bell pepper, seeded and diced

1 large green bell pepper, seeded and diced

1 (28-ounce) can diced tomatoes

1 (15-ounce) can pinto beans, drained and rinsed

12 saffron strands (optional)

1 (10-ounce) package frozen corn, or 1 (11-ounce) can, drained

1¼ cups dry long-grain white rice

1 teaspoon sweet paprika

1 teaspoon ground turmeric

2 to 3 cups Vegetable Broth (page 180), divided

Fresh basil, for garnish (optional)

1. In a large skillet, heat the vinegar over medium-high heat. Add the garlic, onion, and bell peppers and sauté until the onion is tender. Add the tomatoes, pinto beans, and saffron (if using) and cook, stirring occasionally, for 5 minutes more.

2. Add the corn and rice and cook for 5 minutes more.

3. Add the paprika, turmeric, and 1 cup of broth, stir to combine, and cook until the rice is tender, 20 to 25 minutes, adding more broth as needed to keep the rice from getting dry. Remove from the heat and garnish with fresh basil, if using. Serve.

SWAP IT: You can use any kind of rice in this dish. But note that you'll need to adjust the cooking time and amount of broth accordingly.

PER SERVING (2 CUPS): Calories: 437; Saturated Fat: 0g; Total Fat: 3g; Protein: 15g; Total Carbs: 91g; Fiber: 14g; Sodium: 472mg

VEGETABLE LENTIL LOAF

PREP TIME: 10 minutes | **COOK TIME:** 40 minutes | **MAKES:** 8 slices | Gluten-free, Nut-free, Soy-free

Lentils and mushrooms are a match made in heaven. Together they become the perfect meatless ground "beef" made from whole foods. My family thinks this recipe is hilarious because when I was growing up I hated meatloaf, but I've never met a lentil loaf I didn't love. What can I say? Plants!

Vegetable oil spray
  (optional)
1 (15-ounce) can lentils,
  drained and rinsed, or
  1½ cups cooked lentils
2 cups diced portobello
  mushrooms
1 cup rolled oats
1 cup finely diced onion
¼ cup ground flaxseed
½ teaspoon ground ginger
¼ teaspoon ground
  white pepper
¾ cup BBQ Sauce
  (page 189), **divided**

1. Preheat the oven to 400°F. Lightly grease a 5-by-9-inch loaf pan with vegetable oil spray or line it with parchment paper.

2. In a large bowl, combine the lentils, mushrooms, oats, onion, ground flaxseed, ginger, and pepper. Using a potato masher or your hands, mash everything together. Pour ½ cup of BBQ sauce into the bowl and mix well with a wooden spoon or spatula.

3. Transfer the mixture to the prepared pan, smoothing it into an even thickness and pushing it into the corners. Pour the remaining ¼ cup of BBQ sauce over the top and spread it out evenly.

4. Bake for 40 minutes, or until the edges of the loaf are browned and pulling away from the pan. Remove from the oven and let cool for 10 minutes.

5. Remove from the pan, cut the lentil loaf into 8 slices with a sharp serrated knife, and serve.

MAKE AHEAD: To prepare this in advance, line the loaf pan with parchment paper, add the lentil mixture, and freeze for about 1 hour. Remove the loaf from the pan and store it in a zip-top plastic bag or airtight container in the freezer for up to 3 months. Thaw in a parchment-lined loaf pan before baking.

INGREDIENT TIP: Use 1½ cups cooked beans instead of canned.

PER SERVING (1 SLICE): Calories: 177; Saturated Fat: 0g; Total Fat: 2g; Protein: 7g; Total Carbs: 34g; Fiber: 6g; Sodium: 71mg

SPLIT PEA KITCHARI

PREP TIME: 15 minutes | **COOK TIME:** 1 hour | **SERVES:** 4 | Gluten-free, Nut-free, Soy-free

Kitchari is a healing Ayurvedic dish that is also comforting, nutritious, and delicious. My version focuses less on tradition and more on the healthy ingredients. Bonus: It's easy to prepare. It's also my go-to for bulk cooking because I can reheat and eat it throughout the week, and it freezes beautifully.

½ cup dried split green or
   yellow peas
½ cup dry basmati rice
1 cup diced red onion
1 cup chopped carrots
1 cup diced potatoes
1 cup diced summer squash
   or winter squash
1 teaspoon ground turmeric
1 teaspoon cumin seed
1 teaspoon coriander seed
1 teaspoon fennel seeds
1 (3-inch) fresh ginger,
   peeled and minced
Juice of 1 large lemon
½ teaspoon freshly ground
   black pepper

1. Combine the split peas and rice in a medium bowl, cover with 2 cups water, and soak for 20 minutes.

2. Drain and rinse the peas and rice and transfer to a large saucepan. Add 3 cups water and bring to a boil over medium-high heat. Lower the heat to medium-low and cook for 20 minutes.

3. Add the onion, carrots, potatoes, and squash, stir to combine, and cook until the rice is tender, 20 to 30 minutes more.

4. While the rice and beans are cooking, in a small skillet, combine the turmeric, cumin, coriander, and fennel seeds and sauté over medium-high heat until aromatic, about 5 minutes. Transfer the seeds to the saucepan, add the ginger, lemon juice, and pepper and stir to combine. Spoon into bowls and serve.

SWAP IT: To keep this fresh and exciting, consider using red lentils or mung beans in place of the split peas, and 3 cups of your choice of vegetables.

PER SERVING (2 CUPS): Calories: 242; Saturated Fat: 0g; Total Fat: 2g; Protein: 10g; Total Carbs: 49g; Fiber: 10g; Sodium: 33mg

REFRIED JACKFRUIT TOSTADAS

PREP TIME: 10 minutes | **COOK TIME:** 20 minutes | **SERVES:** 2 | Gluten-free, Nut-free, Soy-free | Quick

Taco or tostada nights happen far more often than just Tuesdays in our household. They are just so easy to pull together. Combining jackfruit with smashed beans creates a creamy, "meaty" topping perfect for this recipe. Make sure to buy water-packed or brined jackfruit, not the kind in syrup.

1 (14-ounce) can jackfruit, drained and rinsed

1 (14-ounce) can vegetarian refried beans

½ cup fresh or jarred salsa

¼ cup nutritional yeast

2 teaspoons chili powder

4 (6-inch) corn tortillas

3 tablespoons aquafaba

(see page 178)

1. Preheat the oven to 400°F. Line a baking sheet with parchment paper.

2. In a medium saucepan, combine the jackfruit, beans, salsa, and ¼ cup water and bring to a boil over medium-high heat. Lower the heat, cover, and simmer for 10 minutes.

3. In a small bowl, combine the nutritional yeast and chili powder. Set aside.

4. Brush both sides of the tortillas with the aquafaba. Place the tortillas on the prepared baking sheet. Spoon about 1 cup of the bean mixture on each tortilla and spread it out. Sprinkle 1 tablespoon of the nutritional yeast mixture over each.

5. Bake for 10 minutes. Serve immediately.

SWAP IT: Not into canned refried beans? Use a can of any red bean, drained and rinsed (or 2 cups cooked beans), and add a chopped hot chile. While cooking for 10 minutes as instructed in step 2, use a potato masher to combine.

PER SERVING (2 TOSTADAS): Calories: 517; Saturated Fat: 1g; Total Fat: 4g; Protein: 23g; Total Carbs: 106g; Fiber: 17g; Sodium: 451mg

YELLOW SPLIT PEA POLENTA

PREP TIME: 10 minutes | **COOK TIME:** 40 minutes | **SERVES:** 6 | Gluten-free, Soy-free | One-pot

You may think of polenta as the prepared stuff you buy in a tube—and there's nothing wrong with that—but it's actually made from dried cornmeal and is traditionally served in a bowl, like porridge or grits. By adding yellow split peas to this recipe, the dish becomes hearty enough to be served as a protein-rich entrée. Serve it simply on its own, or with steamed, stir-fried, or roasted vegetables for a well-rounded and satisfying meal.

1 cup full-fat or light
   coconut milk
3 cups Vegetable Broth
   (page 180)
3 garlic cloves, minced
2 teaspoons Spicy Umami
   Blend (page 196)
½ teaspoon ground
   turmeric
½ teaspoon ground cumin
½ cup dried polenta or
   cornmeal
½ cup dried yellow
   split peas
2 tablespoons
   nutritional yeast
1 teaspoon lemon juice

1. In a large saucepan, combine the coconut milk, broth, garlic, umami blend, turmeric, and cumin and bring to a boil over medium-high heat. While whisking continuously, slowly pour in the polenta and whisk until it has been completely incorporated and there are no lumps. Lower the heat to low and simmer, whisking often, until the polenta starts to thicken, about 5 minutes. The polenta should still be slightly loose.

2. Cover and cook for 30 minutes, whisking every 5 to 6 minutes. When the polenta becomes too thick to whisk, switch to stirring it with a wooden spoon. The polenta is done when its texture is creamy and the individual grains are tender.

3. Remove from the heat and gently stir in the peas, nutritional yeast, and lemon juice. Cover and let sit for 5 minutes to thicken the polenta before serving.

SMART SHOPPING: Both cornmeal and yellow split peas can be purchased in bulk and stored in jars in your pantry.

PER SERVING (1 CUP): Calories: 173; Saturated Fat: 7g; Total Fat: 9g; Protein: 6g; Total Carbs: 20g; Fiber: 5g; Sodium: 12mg

GLAZED PINEAPPLE "HAM"

PREP TIME: 15 minutes | **COOK TIME:** 1 hour | **SERVES:** 4 | Nut-free

Seitan (SAY-tan)—also known as "wheat meat"—is believed to have been created by Buddhist monks trying to encourage followers to adopt a vegetarian diet. Translated from Japanese, seitan means "ideal protein"—and translated into my kitchen, it means anything you can eat, I can eat vegan! It's actually quite easy to make, so don't let the number of ingredients intimidate you. This variation is "ham" flavored, which is terrific for a variety of holidays.

FOR THE SEITAN

¾ cup vital wheat gluten
1 tablespoon rolled oats
1 tablespoon chickpea flour
1 tablespoon
  nutritional yeast
1 teaspoon chipotle
  chile powder
1 teaspoon tomato powder
½ teaspoon smoked paprika
¼ teaspoon ground cloves
¼ teaspoon garlic powder
¼ teaspoon freshly ground
  black pepper
½ cup Vegetable Broth
  (page 180)
1 tablespoon low-sodium
  soy sauce
1 tablespoon pure
  maple syrup

FOR THE GLAZE

1 (8-ounce) can pineapple
  chunks in juice, drained
  (juice reserved)
2 teaspoons tomato powder
½ teaspoon smoked paprika

TO MAKE THE SEITAN

1. Preheat the oven to 375°F.

2. In a large bowl or in the bowl of a stand mixer fitted with the dough hook, combine the vital wheat gluten, oats, chickpea flour, nutritional yeast, chipotle powder, tomato powder, smoked paprika, cloves, garlic powder, and pepper. Add the broth, soy sauce, and maple syrup and mix until well combined. Knead for 5 minutes, until the mixture has a slightly tacky consistency similar to bread dough. Form the mixture into a log resembling a roast. Wrap the log in parchment paper and then in aluminum foil. Bake for 45 minutes.

TO MAKE THE GLAZE

3. In a food processor, combine the pineapple, tomato powder, and paprika and purée until thick and pourable. Drizzle in a little of the reserved pineapple juice as needed until it reaches the desired consistency. Pour the remaining pineapple juice into a shallow baking pan.

4. Carefully remove the foil and parchment from the seitan and transfer the seitan to the baking pan. Brush the pineapple glaze over the seitan ham. Return the seitan to the oven and bake for 15 minutes more.

5. Transfer the seitan to a wire rack and let rest for 15 minutes before slicing and serving. To store, place the seitan in a zip-top plastic bag or airtight container, cover with vegetable broth, and freeze for up to 3 months.

INGREDIENT TIP: You can use a mandoline to cut very thin pieces of the seitan before storing it in the broth. Once they are thawed, you can use them as vegan prosciutto or for sandwiches.

PER SERVING (2 SLICES): Calories: 154; Saturated Fat: 0g; Total Fat: 1g; Protein: 21g; Total Carbs: 17g; Fiber: 2g; Sodium: 139mg

TURMERIC TEMPEH STIR-FRY

PREP TIME: 10 minutes | **COOK TIME:** 15 minutes | **SERVES:** 2 | Gluten-free option, Nut-free | Quick

Here you are—the go-to stir-fry you've been waiting for. Though tempeh is the star here, tofu works great instead, and so does seitan. There's a lot of flexibility with the spices, too, though those in this recipe lean toward an Asian flavor profile. If you use balsamic vinegar and oregano, basil, and parsley, you can turn this into an Italian-style meal. Serve with a side of rice if you'd like!

1 (8-ounce) package tempeh, cut into 16 cubes

1 tablespoon minced garlic

1 tablespoon unseasoned rice vinegar

1 tablespoon low-sodium soy sauce or tamari

1 teaspoon ground cinnamon

1 teaspoon ground turmeric

1 teaspoon ground cumin

1 teaspoon chili powder

2 large carrots, diced

1 large red bell pepper, seeded and sliced

1 large yellow bell pepper, seeded and sliced

6 ounces kale, leaves stemmed and chopped

2 teaspoons arrowroot powder

1. Place the tempeh in a medium bowl. Set aside.

2. In a small bowl, combine the garlic, vinegar, soy sauce, cinnamon, turmeric, cumin, and chili powder and whisk until combined. Pour the mixture over the tempeh and let sit for 5 minutes.

3. Drain the tempeh, reserving the marinade.

4. In a large skillet or wok, cook the tempeh over medium heat, stirring, until it begins to brown, 4 to 6 minutes. Add the carrots, bell peppers, and kale and cook, stirring, until the kale has brightened in color and the carrots are tender, 3 to 5 minutes.

5. Whisk the arrowroot into the reserved marinade until smooth. Pour the mixture into the skillet, stir to combine, and simmer for just 3 minutes more.

6. Divide the tempeh mixture between two plates, drizzle with the thickened marinade, and serve.

MAKE AHEAD: Complete steps 1 and 2 and marinate the tempeh in an airtight container overnight or up to 3 days. That extra-long marinating makes it so tender!

ALLERGEN TIP: Be sure to use gluten-free tempeh and tamari.

PER SERVING (1 CUP): Calories: 378; Saturated Fat: 3g; Total Fat: 14g; Protein: 28g; Total Carbs: 43g; Fiber: 10g; Sodium: 395mg

HEART-OF-PALM CAKES

PREP TIME: 15 minutes | **COOK TIME:** 25 minutes | **MAKES:** 8 patties | Gluten-free option, Nut-free, Soy-free option

Flaky hearts of palm and meaty jackfruit deliver texture in this play on crab cakes. The umami flavor is developed from start (vinegar) to finish (smoked paprika) and everywhere in between (briny vegetables, mushrooms, and homemade mustard).

¼ cup balsamic vinegar

½ cup diced sweet onion

1 cup diced mushrooms

1 (15-ounce) can jackfruit, drained and rinsed

1 (14-ounce) can or jar hearts of palm, drained

¼ cup Boozy Brown Mustard (page 188)

1 tablespoon arrowroot powder

2 teaspoons Spicy Umami Blend (page 196), or 1 teaspoon salt

¾ cup panko bread crumbs, divided

½ cup Tofu Sour Cream (page 181; optional)

1 teaspoon smoked paprika

1. Preheat the oven to 400°F. Line a baking sheet with parchment paper or a silicone baking mat.

2. In a large skillet, heat the vinegar over medium-high heat until it just begins to bubble. Add the onion and mushrooms and cook until the onion softens, 3 to 5 minutes. Remove the skillet from the heat and set aside to cool.

3. Coarsely chop the jackfruit and hearts of palm and transfer them to a large bowl. Add the mustard, arrowroot, umami blend, mushroom mixture, and ¼ cup of panko and stir until combined.

4. Divide the mixture into 8 portions and shape them into small, slider-style patties. Place the remaining ½ cup of panko in a shallow bowl. Coat the patties with the panko and transfer them to the prepared baking sheet. Bake for 20 minutes, or until golden.

5. Serve topped with a dollop of sour cream, if desired, and a couple of pinches of smoked paprika.

SWAP IT: In place of jackfruit, chop up some canned artichoke hearts in a food processor to get that stringy, meaty texture.

ALLERGEN TIP: For gluten-free use gluten-free bread crumbs instead of panko. For soy-free use plain coconut or pea yogurt instead of the Tofu Sour Cream.

PER SERVING (2 PATTIES): Calories: 135; Saturated Fat: 0g; Total Fat: 1g; Protein: 3g; Total Carbs: 28g; Fiber: 2g; Sodium: 234mg

MUSHROOM SLOPPY JOES

PREP TIME: 10 minutes | **COOK TIME:** 10 minutes | **MAKES:** 8 | Gluten-free option, Nut-free option, Soy-free option | One-pot, Quick

Textured vegetable protein, known as TVP, is one of my favorite ingredients for making wholesome vegan ground "meat" dishes. Made from soy flour, it's got a chewy texture and absorbs whatever flavors you cook with. Bonus: It's a great source of protein, too. This is one of those recipes you can serve to your nonvegan family or friends and they will love it. I promise.

½ cup diced onion

1 cup diced mushrooms

½ teaspoon ground cumin

½ teaspoon garlic powder

½ teaspoon Spicy Umami Blend (page 196)

¼ teaspoon smoked paprika

½ cup unsweetened plant-based milk

1 cup TVP

½ cup Vegetable Broth (page 180)

½ teaspoon freshly ground black pepper

4 whole-grain hamburger buns, toasted

1. In a large skillet, combine the onion and mushrooms and dry sauté over medium-high heat, stirring frequently, until the onion softens, about 3 minutes. Add the cumin, garlic powder, umami blend, paprika, and plant-based milk and bring to a light boil. Add the TVP and broth, stir well, cover, and cook until the liquid has been absorbed, about 10 minutes. Add the pepper and stir to combine.

2. Spoon the mixture onto the hamburger buns and serve.

ALLERGEN TIP: You can use 2 to 3 cups frozen meatless crumbles in place of the TVP for a soy-free option. To make it gluten-free, use gluten-free hamburger buns or serve the sloppy joe in a bowl like a stew. If you are sensitive to nuts, use unsweetened seed milk.

PER SERVING (1 SLOPPY JOE): Calories: 110; Saturated Fat: 0g; Total Fat: 1g; Protein: 9g; Total Carbs: 15g; Fiber: 3g; Sodium: 114mg

CHAPTER 8

SNACKS AND TREATS

BEET CHIPS

PREP TIME: 15 minutes | **COOK TIME:** 20 minutes | **SERVES:** 4 | Gluten-free, Nut-free, Soy-free | Quick

Beets: People seem to love 'em or hate 'em. I love them in cold salads and in soups—but my husband was not a fan. Well, not until I started preparing them like potato chips! I recommend using a mandoline to get the thinnest slices possible.

4 medium beets, scrubbed

3 tablespoons aquafaba
  (see page 178)

1 teaspoon dried dill

1 teaspoon dried chives

1 teaspoon dried parsley

1 teaspoon cayenne pepper

1. Preheat the oven to 375°F. Line two baking sheets with parchment paper or silicone baking mats.

2. Using a mandoline or a very sharp knife, cut the beets into $1/16$-inch-thick slices. Transfer to a large bowl.

3. Add the aquafaba, dill, chives, parsley, and cayenne and toss until evenly coated.

4. Arrange the beet slices in a single layer on the prepared baking sheets and bake for 15 minutes, until they begin to curl and crisp.

APPLIANCE TIP: Air fryer fans, this one's for you! Preheat your air fryer to 400°F. Transfer the beet slices to an unlined air fryer basket and cook for 8 minutes, shaking every 2 minutes, until crispy.

PER SERVING (2 CUPS): Calories: 38; Saturated Fat: 0g; Total Fat: 0g; Protein: 1g; Total Carbs: 8g; Fiber: 3g; Sodium: 64mg

CHEESY KALE CHIPS

PREP TIME: 5 minutes | **COOK TIME:** 20 minutes | **MAKES:** 8 cups | Gluten-free option, Nut-free | 5-ingredient, Quick

Oh, kale chips, you're just *so vegan*. But turning this leafy green into a crunchy snack is genius, and whoever invited it should earn a medal. You can really have fun with a world of flavors by swapping out vinegar and soy sauce with other flavorful liquids such as red wine vinegar and hot sauce for Mexican chips, white wine vinegar and curry paste for Indian chips, and balsamic vinegar and BBQ sauce for Italian chips.

8 cups torn stemmed
  kale leaves
1 teaspoon rice vinegar
1 teaspoon low-sodium soy
  sauce or tamari
3 tablespoons nutritional
  yeast, divided

1. Preheat the oven to 275°F. Line two baking sheets with parchment paper or silicone baking mats.

2. In a large bowl, combine the kale, vinegar, soy sauce, and 2 tablespoons of nutritional yeast and toss until evenly coated. Using your hands, massage the ingredients into the kale for about 2 minutes.

3. Transfer the kale to the prepared baking sheets, arranging it in a single layer. Bake for 20 minutes, or until crisp, gently shaking the pan and tossing the chips with tongs after 10 minutes.

4. Sprinkle the remaining 1 tablespoon of nutritional yeast over the kale chips, shake the pan to coat, and transfer to a bowl. Serve immediately. Store leftover chips in an airtight container at room temperature for up to 3 days (see Tip).

STORAGE TIP: Kale chips are made to be eaten. Now. But if you must cook them in advance, store them well. I have tried a variety of ways, and I'm here to say the *best* way is in a large mason jar at room temperature for no more than 2 to 3 days. To "spruce" them up to get a bit of crunch back, use your air fryer or bake at 275°F for 8 to 10 minutes.

ALLERGEN TIP: For a gluten-free version, use tamari labeled "gluten-free."

PER SERVING (2 CUPS): Calories: 32; Saturated Fat: 0g; Total Fat: 0g; Protein: 3g; Total Carbs: 4g; Fiber: 1g; Sodium: 53mg

KALE CHICKPEA DIP

PREP TIME: 15 minutes | **COOK TIME:** 25 minutes | **SERVES:** 6 | Gluten-free, Nut-free, Soy-free option | Quick

This is a nourishing take on spinach dip, which traditionally features up to five heavy dairy products. This version showcases nutrient-dense kale to hold the thick and creamy bean-based purée together beautifully. Serve it as a dip with raw vegetables or crackers or as a spread on fresh baked bread or toasted sourdough. Or be like me and dollop it over Yellow Split Pea Polenta (page 145). It's really good—trust me!

1 cup thinly sliced red onion

2 teaspoons minced garlic

4 cups tightly packed chopped stemmed kale leaves

1 (15-ounce) can or jar quartered artichokes, drained

1 (15 ounce) can chickpeas, drained and rinsed

1 cup Tofu Sour Cream (page 181)

¼ cup nutritional yeast

1 teaspoon Spicy Umami Blend (page 196), **or** ½ teaspoon salt

¼ teaspoon freshly ground black pepper

1. Preheat the oven to 350°F.

2. In a large skillet, combine the onion, garlic, and kale and sauté over medium-high heat, stirring frequently, until the onion softens and the kale turns deep green, for 5 minutes.

3. In a food processor, combine the artichokes and chickpeas and pulse until chunky and just beginning to become smooth and creamy. Transfer the chickpea mixture to the skillet.

4. Add the sour cream, nutritional yeast, umami blend, and pepper to the skillet and stir until well combined.

5. Transfer the mixture to a 1-quart baking dish and bake for 25 to 30 minutes, until bubbling and golden brown. Remove from the oven and serve.

SWAP IT: Though I love kale in this for the texture, you can absolutely use spinach. Or arugula, or Swiss chard, or . . . you get the point: any leafy green will do.

ALLERGEN TIP: Use plain soy-free vegan yogurt instead of the Tofu Sour Cream.

PER SERVING (½ CUP): Calories: 179; Saturated Fat: 1g; Total Fat: 6g; Protein: 12g; Total Carbs: 23g; Fiber: 8g; Sodium: 181mg

SUPER-GREEN GUACAMOLE

PREP TIME: 10 minutes | **SERVES:** 4 | Gluten-free, Nut-free, Soy-free | No-cook, Quick

This isn't really guacamole but it's inspired by it. Sure, you can dip raw veggies, crackers, or pita bread into it as an appetizer, but don't miss the chance to wrap it up in a tortilla or collard leaf and serve it as a handheld treat. Or use it as a sandwich spread, a filling for a split baked sweet potato, or a topping for soups, chili, or nachos in place of sour cream.

8 ounces kale, leaves stemmed and chopped

8 ounces fresh spinach

1 (10-ounce) package frozen peas, thawed

1 small jalapeño, seeded and coarsely chopped

1 ripe avocado, halved and pitted

3 tablespoons lime juice

¼ teaspoon kosher salt, or ½ teaspoon Spicy Umami Blend (page 196)

2 green onions, chopped

1. In a food processor, combine the kale, spinach, peas, and jalapeño and pulse until coarsely chopped.

2. Scoop the avocado into the food processor, add the lime juice, and pulse until well blended and creamy, with flecks of kale and spinach still visible. Transfer to a serving bowl.

3. Sprinkle the salt over the guacamole, top with the green onions, and serve.

STORAGE TIP: We're using avocado here, folks, which is the *best*, so you're going to want to eat this all up! But if you happen to have leftovers or if you made this specifically as a sandwich spread, save the juiced limes you used. Transfer the guacamole to an airtight container. Slice the juiced limes and place them directly onto the guacamole. This will help keep it from browning, but you should still finish the guac within 3 days.

PER SERVING (1 CUP): Calories: 167; Saturated Fat: 2g; Total Fat: 9g; Protein: 8g; Total Carbs: 20g; Fiber: 10g; Sodium: 72mg

ONCE-BAKED PAPRIKA POTATOES

PREP TIME: 10 minutes | **COOK TIME:** 30 minutes | **SERVES:** 4 | Gluten-free, Nut-free, Soy-free option

This recipe produces twice-baked potatoes with one bake. The secret is to use small potatoes that you steam before putting in the oven.

4 small russet potatoes, scrubbed

¼ cup Tofu Sour Cream (page 181)

1 teaspoon Boozy Brown Mustard (page 188)

2 teaspoons nutritional yeast

½ teaspoon ground turmeric

1 teaspoon smoked paprika

1. Preheat the oven to 400°F. Line a baking sheet with parchment paper or a silicone baking mat.

2. Fill a large saucepan with about 1 inch of water, insert a steamer basket, and bring to a boil over high heat. Lower the heat to medium-high and place the potatoes in the steamer. Cover and steam for 12 to 15 minutes, until the potatoes are tender.

3. Remove the potatoes from the steamer and set aside until cool enough to handle, then cut each potato in half lengthwise. Gently scoop the flesh from the potato halves, leaving about ¼ inch of flesh attached to the skins, and place it in a medium bowl. Place the potato skins on the prepared baking sheet and set aside.

4. Add the sour cream, mustard, nutritional yeast, and turmeric to the bowl with the potatoes and use a potato masher to mash the mixture until creamy.

5. Spoon the mashed potatoes into the potato skins and sprinkle pinches of paprika over each potato half. Bake for 15 minutes. Serve immediately.

APPLIANCE TIP: Multicooker friends, place the potatoes in the pot and cook on low pressure for 10 minutes before moving on to step 3.

ALLERGEN TIP: To make this soy-free, use plain coconut or pea yogurt instead of the Tofu Sour Cream.

PER SERVING (2 HALVES): Calories: 156; Saturated Fat: 0g; Total Fat: 1g; Protein: 6g; Total Carbs: 31g; Fiber: 3g; Sodium: 17mg

BBQ BAKED FRENCH FRIES

PREP TIME: 10 minutes | **COOK TIME:** 35 minutes | **SERVES:** 2 to 4 | Gluten-free, Nut-free, Soy-free

Crunchy and tender roasted potatoes are awesome, and seasoned potatoes, even more so. We make homemade fries at least twice a week—and not just as a side. Spoon a cup or two of Three-Bean Chili (page 106) over them, add a drizzle of Cheesy Chickpea Sauce (page 194), and you've got yourself an entrée of plant-based chili cheese fries.

2 large russet potatoes, scrubbed

½ teaspoon pure maple syrup

1 teaspoon paprika

1 teaspoon garlic powder

½ teaspoon freshly ground black pepper

½ teaspoon ground mustard

½ teaspoon chipotle chile powder

½ teaspoon smoked paprika

¼ teaspoon chili powder

1 tablespoon arrowroot powder, potato starch, or chickpea flour (optional)

1 teaspoon Spicy Umami Blend (page 196)

1. Preheat the oven to 450°F. Line a baking sheet with parchment paper or a silicone baking mat.

2. Cut the potatoes into ¼-inch-thick slices and then into ¼-inch-wide strips. Transfer the fries to a large bowl, cover them in 3 to 4 cups water, and soak for 20 minutes. Drain the potatoes, rinse, and pat dry, then transfer them to a large bowl.

3. Drizzle the maple syrup over the potatoes. Add the paprika, garlic powder, pepper, ground mustard, chipotle powder, paprika, chili powder, and arrowroot and toss until evenly coated.

4. Transfer the potatoes to the prepared baking sheet and bake for 30 to 35 minutes, until golden.

5. Season with the umami blend while hot, then serve.

APPLIANCE TIP: If you have an air fryer, you can get a bit closer to that crunchy fried feeling you're looking for. Toss the potatoes in 3 tablespoons aquafaba (see page 178) when adding the maple syrup, *definitely* use the starchy arrowroot, and air-fry on 400°F for 20 to 25 minutes.

PER SERVING (2 CUPS): Calories: 313; Saturated Fat: 0g; Total Fat: 1g; Protein: 9g; Total Carbs: 71g; Fiber: 6g; Sodium: 31mg

PICKLED CUCUMBERS

PREP TIME: 10 minutes, plus overnight chilling | **COOK TIME:** 5 minutes | **SERVES:** 4 |
Gluten-free option, Nut-free, Soy-free option

Pickled vegetables are an umami go-to. They can be a bit more challenging if you want to make them salt-free (no salt = no brine) and sugar-free, though in this recipe I'm skipping the sugar altogether and turning to seaweed and soy sauce to get that briny flavor. Try them straight out of the jar as fun snack, dice them up to make an Asian-style relish to serve with Creamy Riced Veggie Wraps (page 90) or Umami Oat Burgers (page 120), or add some to Chick(pea) Pecan Salad (page 79).

1 (2-inch) strip kombu
2 cups rice vinegar
½ cup low-sodium soy
   sauce or tamari
1 tablespoon dried dill
1 teaspoon whole cloves
½ teaspoon red
   pepper flakes
2 small cucumbers (about
   1 pound), cut into ¼-inch-
   thick rounds
1 small white onion, halved
   and thinly sliced

1. In a small saucepan, combine the kombu, vinegar, soy sauce or tamari, dill, cloves, and red pepper flakes and bring to a boil over medium-high heat. Remove from the heat and set aside.

2. Place the cucumbers and onion in a 1-quart glass jar. Pour the hot vinegar mixture into the jar and use a spoon to push the cucumbers completely under the liquid. Cover with a lid and refrigerate overnight before serving. The pickles can be stored in the refrigerator for up to 1 week.

INGREDIENT TIP: If you're eating a totally salt-free diet, you might find the combination of kombu and soy sauce a bit much (not me!). If so, simply omit the kombu.

ALLERGEN TIP: To make this gluten-free, be sure to use a tamari labeled "gluten-free" or coconut aminos, which will also make this dish soy-free.

PER SERVING (½ CUP): Calories: 40; Saturated Fat: 0g; Total Fat: 0g; Protein: 2g; Total Carbs: 8g; Fiber: 1g; Sodium: 149mg

MUSHROOM PÂTÉ

PREP TIME: 40 minutes, plus 1 hour chilling | **COOK TIME:** 8 minutes | **MAKES:** 3 cups | Gluten-free, Soy-free

By now, it's likely you're hip to my ways . . .

Umami rocks
The easier, the better
Re-creating nonvegan foods is my favorite

. . . which is exactly what this incredibly simple approach to a rich (and dare I say it—fancy) pâté is all about.

½ cup cashews
1 cup boiling water
¼ cup balsamic vinegar
2 cups sliced baby bella
  mushrooms
1 small sweet onion,
  quartered
½ cup Plant Pesto
  (page 185)

1. In a small bowl, combine the cashews and the boiling water and let sit for 30 minutes.

2. In a small skillet, combine the vinegar, mushrooms, and onion and sauté over medium-high heat until the onion softens, 5 to 8 minutes. Set aside.

3. Drain the cashews and transfer them to a food processor. Add the mushroom-onion mixture and pulse until creamy and thick. Slowly drizzle in water 1 tablespoon at a time, if needed, to make it creamy.

4. Transfer the mushroom mixture to a bowl, add the pesto, and stir until well combined.

5. Serve at room temperature, or cover and refrigerate for at least 1 hour, then serve cold. The pâté can be stored in an airtight container in the refrigerator for up to 5 days.

SWAP IT: I like baby bellas (also known as creminis) because they are at that mid-range of price and flavor. I adore shiitakes, but they are pricey. White or button mushrooms are A-OK, too.

PER SERVING (½ CUP): Calories: 142; Saturated Fat: 1g; Total Fat: 7g; Protein: 4g; Total Carbs: 13g; Fiber: 1g; Sodium: 123mg

ENDURANCE BARS

PREP TIME: 10 minutes, plus 30 minutes chilling | **COOK TIME:** 45 minutes | **MAKES:** 9 bars | Gluten-free

My husband, a swim and triathlon coach, and I came up with this recipe for a cooking class focused on how to fuel up during a long endurance workout or hike. It's filled with carbs and protein. We recommend wrapping each bar individually so you can stuff one in your backpack, cycling jersey, or shorts pocket.

½ cup dry sweet brown rice

1 tablespoon ground
  chia seeds

3 tablespoons warm water

8 ounces Tempeh "Bacon"
  (page 183)

½ cup walnuts

2 tablespoons liquid aminos

2 tablespoons pure
  maple syrup

1. Line an 8-inch square baking pan with parchment paper.

2. In a medium saucepan, combine the rice and 2 cups water and bring to a boil over medium-high heat. Lower the heat to low, cover, and simmer for 45 minutes. Remove from the heat and let sit, covered, for 10 minutes.

3. In a small bowl or measuring cup, whisk together the chia seeds and warm water. Set aside.

4. In a food processor, combine the tempeh bacon and walnuts and pulse until coarsely chopped, with some chunks remaining. Transfer to a medium bowl.

5. Add the rice, chia mixture, liquid aminos, and maple syrup to the tempeh mixture and stir to combine well.

6. Transfer the rice mixture to the prepared baking pan and press it into an even layer with a spatula. Cover and refrigerate for at least 30 minutes.

7. Cut into bars and wrap individually in parchment paper or place in individual storage bags.

SWAP IT: White sushi rice is delicious in this, and cooks faster than brown rice. Short-grain brown rice is also a fine substitute, but you'll want to toss it with a little rice vinegar or mirin to get the proper texture for these bars.

PER SERVING (1 BAR): Calories: 174; Saturated Fat: 1g; Total Fat: 8g; Protein: 7g; Total Carbs: 19g; Fiber: 1g; Sodium: 40mg

BANANA BULGUR BARS

PREP TIME: 10 minutes | **COOK TIME:** 30 minutes | **MAKES 9 BARS** | Soy-free

Fruit-and-grain bars are a great treat to satisfy your sweet tooth *and* they happen to be a healthy carb-filled snack, perfect for the kids to eat after school. And yep, they're a mighty fine option for breakfast on the go, too. The surprising star of these bars is the bulgur—1 dry cup boasts 17 grams of protein!

2 ripe large bananas

1 tablespoon pure
  maple syrup

½ teaspoon pure
  vanilla extract

1 cup rolled oats

1 cup medium-grind or
  coarse bulgur

¼ cup chopped walnuts

1. Preheat the oven to 350°F. Line an 8-inch square baking pan with parchment paper.

2. In a medium bowl, mash the bananas with a fork. Add the maple syrup and vanilla and mix well. Add the oats, bulgur, and walnuts and mix until combined.

3. Transfer the mixture to the prepared baking pan and bake for 25 to 30 minutes, until the top is crispy.

4. Let cool completely, then cut into 9 bars and transfer to an airtight container or a large zip-top plastic bag. Store at room temperature for up to 5 days.

PAIR IT: Serve this for dessert with a scoop of vegan ice cream or Cherry Nice Cream (page 167).

PER SERVING (1 BAR): Calories: 142; Saturated Fat: 0g; Total Fat: 3g; Protein: 4g; Total Carbs: 26g; Fiber: 4g; Sodium: 3mg

CINNAMON-AND-SPICE GRANOLA

PREP TIME: 10 minutes | **COOK TIME:** 30 minutes | **SERVES:** 6 | Gluten-free, Soy-free

This recipe can be used as a cereal, dessert topping (hello, Chocolatey Mousse, page 169), or quick snack by the handful. That's the beauty of granola, and home-made is even better. Whole chia seeds and a little maple syrup help all the ingredients cling together and cluster into perfect little bites of grains, fruit, and nuts.

3 cups rolled oats

1 cup unsweetened
   dried apples

¾ cup chopped pecans

2 tablespoons chia seeds

1 teaspoon ground
   cinnamon

½ teaspoon ground nutmeg

¼ cup pure maple syrup or
   agave syrup

2 tablespoons extra-virgin
   olive oil (optional; see Tip)

1. Preheat the oven to 300°F. Line a baking sheet with parchment paper or a silicone baking mat.

2. In a large bowl, combine the oats, apples, pecans, chia seeds, cinnamon, nutmeg, maple syrup, and olive oil (if using) and toss well to coat.

3. Pour the mixture onto the prepared baking sheet and spread it evenly with a spatula or your hands. Bake for 25 to 30 minutes, stirring about halfway through, until golden and lightly toasted.

4. Remove from the oven and let cool, then break up any large chunks. Transfer the granola to a large mason jar or six single-serving airtight containers. Store in a cool, dry place or in the refrigerator for up to 2 weeks.

SWAP IT: If omitting the olive oil, increase the maple syrup or agave by 1 to 2 tablespoons or drizzle in a little water to moisten the mixture before baking.

PER SERVING (1 CUP): Calories: 390; Saturated Fat: 2g; Total Fat: 15g; Protein: 11g; Total Carbs: 57g; Fiber: 10g; Sodium: 16mg

CHERRY NICE CREAM

PREP TIME: 10 minutes | **SERVES:** 6 | Gluten-free, Nut-free, Soy-free | 5-ingredient, No-cook, Quick

You scream, I scream, we all scream for "nice" cream! What's more wholesome than skipping the dairy altogether and just whizzing up some frozen fruit as a stand-in for ice cream? Let's be clear: I did not invent the whipped frozen fruit concept, but I stand by my choice of frozen cherries and bananas, which go perfectly together. Feeling sassy? Add ¼ cup dark chocolate chunks or vegan chocolate chips, or a few pieces of Super-Seed Chocolate Bark (page 175).

6 frozen bananas, peeled, cut into chunks

3 cups frozen pitted cherries

1. In a food processor, combine the bananas and cherries and purée, scraping down the sides of the blender jar as needed, until smooth and creamy.

2. Serve immediately.

SWAP IT: Try frozen pineapple, blueberries, blackberries, or mango.

PER SERVING (1 CUP): Calories: 154; Saturated Fat: 0g; Total Fat: 1g; Protein: 2g; Total Carbs: 39g; Fiber: 5g; Sodium: 0mg

CHOCOLATEY MOUSSE

PREP TIME: 10 minutes, plus 1 hour chilling | **SERVES:** 6 | Gluten-free, Nut-free | No-cook

Tofu is a miracle food. It can take on so many amazing flavors—and with just a few ingredients, a block of tofu can even turn into a smooth, sweet treat like this one. The mousse is delightful served in a dessert cup with a little fresh fruit and mint, but don't stop there. Use it to fill a precooked vegan crust to make a tart, add it to a morning smoothie, or dollop it over pancakes or waffles for breakfast.

1 (12-ounce) block firm
  tofu, drained
¼ cup pure maple syrup
¼ cup unsweetened
  cocoa powder
1 teaspoon pure
  vanilla extract
1 cup berries (optional)
¼ cup fresh mint leaves
  (optional)

1. In a food processor, combine the tofu, maple syrup, cocoa powder, and vanilla extract and pulse until smooth and thick. Don't overprocess! Transfer to a bowl and refrigerate for at least 1 hour or up to overnight before serving.

2. Spoon the mousse into dessert bowls and serve topped with fresh berries and mint, if desired.

SWAP IT: While I like a firm tofu, you can absolutely use shelf-stable silken tofu. The texture varies a bit, but it'll work just fine.

PER SERVING (1 CUP): Calories: 126; Saturated Fat: 1g; Total Fat: 5g; Protein: 10g; Total Carbs: 13g; Fiber: 2g; Sodium: 10mg

NUTTY DATE TRUFFLES

PREP TIME: 10 minutes, plus 1 hour chilling | **MAKES:** 12 | Gluten-free, Soy-free | No-cook

Once again, we have proof that many sweet, plant-based foods can show up as dessert. Or breakfast. Or a snack. This recipe is super-easy to make (and to double or triple for entertaining). Unsweetened coconut creates a chewy, cookie-like texture that makes the truffles fluffy and light.

1 cup raw cashews

2 cups boiling water

¾ cup pitted dates

¼ cup gluten-free rolled oats

1 cup unsweetened shredded coconut

2 tablespoons unsweetened cocoa powder

1. Line a baking sheet with parchment paper.

2. In a small bowl, combine the cashews and boiling water and let sit for 30 minutes. Drain the cashews, reserving the soaking water.

3. In a food processor, combine the cashews, dates, oats, coconut, and cocoa powder and pulse until fully combined, adding the reserved cashew soaking water 1 tablespoon at a time as needed to achieve a chunky cookie dough–like texture.

4. Scoop 1 tablespoon of the mixture, form it into a ball, and set it on the prepared baking sheet. Repeat with the remaining mixture.

5. Refrigerate for 1 hour before serving. The truffles can be stored in an airtight container in the refrigerator for up to 5 days.

SWAP IT: Any dried fruit will do. Try dried fruit appropriate to the season (in winter, cranberries + cherries for Christmas stocking stuffers = yes).

PER SERVING (1 TRUFFLE): Calories: 127; Saturated Fat: 3g; Total Fat: 8g; Protein: 3g; Total Carbs: 13g; Fiber: 2g; Sodium: 3mg

STRAWBERRIES AND CREAM

PREP TIME: 10 minutes | **SERVES:** 8 | Gluten-free, Soy-free | 5-ingredient, No-cook, Quick

With cashew cream, you can make a gorgeous dessert in minutes. Fresh basil (or mint) adds a pop of color. Try serving this dessert parfait-style with layers of Cinnamon-and-Spice Granola (page 166) or Chocolatey Mousse (page 169).

1 cup fresh basil leaves
  (optional)
1 pint strawberries, hulled
  and sliced
2 cups Cashew Cream
  (page 182)

1. If using the fresh basil, stack the leaves, starting with the largest on the bottom and building up, then roll up the stack like a cigar. Using a sharp knife, cut the rolled leaves crosswise into ⅛-inch-thick strips (this is known as "chiffonade"). Set aside.

2. Spoon ½ cup of strawberries into each of eight dessert bowls or cups and top each with ¼ cup of cashew cream. Sprinkle the shredded basil over the top and serve immediately.

INGREDIENT TIP: When strawberries aren't in season, frozen ones work great instead. Thaw them in the refrigerator overnight before using.

PER SERVING (1 CUP): Calories: 130; Saturated Fat: 1g; Total Fat: 8g; Protein: 3g; Total Carbs: 12g; Fiber: 2g; Sodium: 3mg

CHUNKY CASHEW NO-BAKE COOKIES

PREP TIME: 15 minutes, plus 1 hour chilling | **COOK TIME:** 5 minutes | **MAKES:** 8 cookies |
Gluten-free, Nut-free option, Soy-free

Quinoa flakes are a nice alternative if you find yourself in an oats rut. Just as oat groats are pressed to create rolled oats, pressed quinoa creates flakes that add a bit more protein punch. To be clear, we're not talking cereal flakes like cornflakes here (though those do exist). Quinoa flakes look a lot like rolled oats, and you can buy them in bulk or packaged under brands such as Ancient Harvest, Sincere Foods, and Shiloh Farms; find them at grocery stores and Walmart.

2 tablespoons pure
maple syrup
2 tablespoons unsweetened
plant-based milk
⅔ cup natural cashew
butter or other nut butter
1 cup quinoa flakes
¼ cup finely chopped raw
cashews (optional)

1. Line a baking sheet with parchment paper.

2. In a saucepan, combine the maple syrup and plant-based milk and cook over medium-high heat until it just begins to bubble.

3. Remove the pan from the heat, add the cashew butter, and stir until well combined. Add the quinoa flakes and chopped cashews (if using) and mix well.

4. Using a cookie scoop or tablespoon, scoop out 2 tablespoons of the mixture and place it on the prepared baking sheet. Repeat with the remaining mixture.

5. Refrigerate for at least 1 hour before serving. The cookies can be stored in an airtight container in the refrigerator for up to 5 days.

SWAP IT: Instant oats work great in place of the quinoa flakes.

ALLERGEN TIP: To make this nut-free, use a seed butter instead of the cashew butter and omit the optional chopped cashews.

PER SERVING (1 COOKIE): Calories: 189; Saturated Fat: 2g; Total Fat: 11g; Protein: 6g; Total Carbs: 18g; Fiber: 0g; Sodium: 4mg

WATERMELON FRIES

PREP TIME: 10 minutes | **SERVES:** 4 | Gluten-free, Nut-free option, Soy-free | No-cook, Quick

We're not frying fruit here (but you know I thought about it for a hot minute). "Fries" refers to the shape of the fruit, but the cinnamon, ginger, and chili powder do provide a level of heat that warms these sweet bites right up! I suggest serving them with a dollop of cashew cream after a big meal, but you can serve them as is, or chop them to use as a topping for salads or even in the Spring Rolls with Pistachio Sauce (page 89) or sushi rolls.

1 small seedless
  watermelon
1 lime, halved
½ teaspoon ground
  cinnamon
½ teaspoon ground ginger
¼ teaspoon chili powder
½ cup Cashew Cream
  (page 182; optional)

1. Cut the watermelon in half. With a sharp knife, cut the end off each half to create flat surfaces. With the large flat side on the bottom, carefully cut off and discard the rind. Cut the watermelon into 1-inch rounds and then cut the rounds into "fries" or sticks. Transfer the fries to a large rimmed baking sheet, arranging them in a single layer.

2. Squeeze the juice from the lime over the fries.

3. In a small bowl, combine the cinnamon, ginger, and chili powder and sprinkle the mixture over the fries. Using tongs, gently toss the fries until evenly coated.

4. Transfer the fries to a large serving bowl. Dollop the cashew cream in the center of the fries, if desired, and serve.

SWAP IT: Use jicama instead of watermelon.

PER SERVING (1 CUP): Calories: 51; Saturated Fat: 0g; Total Fat: 0g; Protein: 1g; Total Carbs: 13g; Fiber: 1g; Sodium: 7mg

SUPER-SEED CHOCOLATE BARK

PREP TIME: 10 minutes | **COOK TIME:** 20 minutes | **SERVES:** 6 to 8 | Gluten-free, Soy-free | 5-ingredient, Quick

Yes, chocolate can be plant-based! Look for cacao percentages between 55 and 85, and read the label to avoid milk-derived ingredients such as casein, milk fat or solids, and whey. Add whatever nuts and seeds you have on hand to the simple melted-chocolate base.

1 cup vegan dark chocolate chips, chunks, or chopped bars
¼ cup chopped unsalted pistachios
1 tablespoon sesame seeds
1 tablespoon raw hulled pumpkin seeds

1. Line a small baking sheet with parchment paper.

2. Fill the bottom of a double boiler or a medium sauce-pan with a few inches of water and bring to a boil over high heat. Lower the heat to medium to keep the water at a simmer. Place the chocolate in the top of the double boiler or in a heatproof bowl that fits over the saucepan (the bottom of the bowl should not touch the water) and place it over the simmering water. Using a silicone spatula, stir frequently until the chocolate has melted. Remove from the heat.

3. In a small bowl, combine the pistachios, sesame seeds, and pumpkin seeds.

4. Scrape the melted chocolate into the center of the prepared baking sheet and spread it into a layer about ¼ inch thick (the chocolate won't cover the entire pan). Sprinkle the seeds over the top. Refrigerator for at least 1 hour before serving.

5. Break the chocolate bark into 10 to 12 rough pieces. Serve immediately or store in an airtight container at room temperature for up to a week or in the refrigerator for up to 2 weeks.

PAIR IT: This is candy, so eat up! You can also crumble it over a Fruity Yogurt Parfait (page 55), or try adding 1/4 cup crumbled bark to the dough for Chunky Cashew No-Bake Cookies (page 172).

PER SERVING (1 PIECE): Calories: 183; Saturated Fat: 6g; Total Fat: 12g; Protein: 3g; Total Carbs: 18g; Fiber: 2g; Sodium: 9mg

CHAPTER 9

HOMEMADE STAPLES

VEGAN EGGS, TWO WAYS

PREP TIME: 5 minutes | **MAKES:** 1 egg | Gluten-free, Nut-free, Soy-free | 5-ingredient, No-cook, Quick

Good news! There are a couple of clever ways to replace eggs using plant-based sources. Flax and chia seeds are perfect for binding cakes, cookies, and bread. Aquafaba is the clever name for something surprising: the liquid from canned chickpeas. Best known as an egg white replacement, it also works to bind ingredients together in some recipes. In this book, I often call for aquafaba as a substitute for oil.

FLAX OR CHIA

1 tablespoon ground
  flaxseed or chia seeds
3 tablespoons warm water

AQUAFABA

3 tablespoons aquafaba

TO MAKE THE FLAX OR CHIA EGG

In a small bowl or measuring cup, whisk together 1 tablespoon ground flaxseed or chia seeds and 3 tablespoons warm water (90° to 110°F) for each egg called for in the recipe. Let stand for 10 minutes before using.

TO MAKE THE AQUAFABA EGG

Drain the liquid from a can of chickpeas and set aside 3 tablespoons for each egg called for in the recipe. Store any remaining aquafaba for later use (see Tip).

INGREDIENT TIP: Whenever you use canned chickpeas, save the aquafaba by pouring it into an ice cube tray and freezing it (each cube is approximately 3 tablespoons liquid). Whenever you need a vegan egg, just thaw out 1 cube.

FLAXSEED

PER SERVING (1 EGG): Calories: 37; Saturated Fat: 0g; Total Fat: 3g; Protein: 1g; Total Carbs: 2g; Fiber: 2g; Sodium: 2mg

CHIA SEED

PER SERVING (1 EGG): Calories: 69; Saturated Fat: 0g; Total Fat: 4g; Protein: 2g; Total Carbs: 6g; Fiber: 5g; Sodium: 2mg

AQUAFABA

PER SERVING (3 TABLESPOONS): Calories: 8; Saturated Fat: 0g; Total Fat: 0g; Protein: 1g; Total Carbs: 1g; Fiber: 0g; Sodium: 0mg

PLANT BUTTER

PREP TIME: 10 minutes | **MAKES:** about 1 cup | Gluten-free, Soy-free option | No-cook, Quick

I have made many versions of vegan butter, and most recipes require a long list of ingredients and a long cooking process. The version I'm sharing here isn't trying to replicate dairy butter, but it does add the characteristics we often look for when we use butter in a recipe: flavor and texture that works with vegetables, bread, sauces, and creams.

½ cup raw cashews

1 cup boiling water

1 tablespoon miso paste

1 tablespoon nutritional yeast

1 teaspoon ground turmeric

1 (5.5-ounce) can coconut milk (¾ cup)

2 teaspoons lemon juice

1. In a small bowl, combine the cashews and boiling water and let sit for 30 minutes. Drain the cashews, reserving the soaking water.

2. Transfer the cashews to a high-speed blender, add the miso, and blend for a few seconds. Add the nutritional yeast and turmeric and blend until combined. Add the coconut milk and lemon juice and blend until creamy and thick with a bit of a shine. If the mixture is too thick, add the reserved cashew soaking water a little bit at a time until the mixture is thick but pourable.

3. Transfer the plant butter to a glass container with a lid, like a mason jar or a 12-ounce round container, cover, and refrigerate for up to 1 week.

ALLERGEN TIP: To make a soy-free version, use chickpea miso paste.

PER SERVING (2 TABLESPOONS): Calories: 101; Saturated Fat: 5g; Total Fat: 9g; Protein: 3g; Total Carbs: 5g; Fiber: 1g; Sodium: 150mg

VEGETABLE BROTH

PREP TIME: 10 minutes | **COOK TIME:** 40 minutes | **MAKES:** 8 cups | Gluten-free, Nut-free, Soy-free | One-pot

I call for a lot of vegetable broth in this book, using it as a replacement for both meat-based broths and oil. You might as well make your own so you always have it on hand (plus, it will make you feel a bit like a culinary rock star). Whenever I start cooking or reheating a bulk-cooked meal, I have my jar of broth on the counter ready to spoon in as needed. It's a real money saver!

4 large carrots, coarsely chopped

4 celery stalks, coarsely chopped

2 large onions, coarsely chopped

1 cup sliced mushrooms

4 to 6 garlic cloves, unpeeled, halved

2 bay leaves

1 teaspoon dried basil

1 teaspoon dried oregano

1 teaspoon dried parsley

1 teaspoon garlic powder

1 teaspoon kosher salt (optional)

1 teaspoon freshly ground black pepper

1. In a large stockpot, combine all the ingredients and 8 cups water. Stir to combine, then bring to a low boil over high heat. Lower the heat to low and simmer for 40 minutes.

2. Strain the broth through a fine-mesh strainer or cheesecloth and discard the solids.

3. The broth can be stored in an airtight container in the refrigerator for up to 1 week or in the freezer for up to 3 months.

MAKE AHEAD: Make this broth first when you're batch cooking. When meal prepping or reheating prepped meals later in the week, set the jar of broth on the counter and add some whenever you need a little liquid for reheating or a splash of flavor. While you can freeze it if you must, it's much better fresh!

PER SERVING (1 CUP): Calories: 15; Saturated Fat: 0g; Total Fat: 0g; Protein: 1g; Total Carbs: 3g; Fiber: 1g; Sodium: 86mg

TOFU SOUR CREAM

PREP TIME: 5 minutes | **MAKES:** 2 cups | Gluten-free, Nut-free | 5-ingredient, No-cook, Quick

Tofu, an acidic ingredient, and a blender are the only things standing between you and your own perfectly made plant-based version of sour cream. I like firm tofu (it makes a sour cream that practically stands up tall and proud on tacos), but truly any type works perfectly.

1 (14-ounce) block firm tofu, drained

¼ cup lemon juice

2 tablespoons rice vinegar

1 teaspoon minced garlic

1 teaspoon white or yellow miso paste

In a blender or food processor, combine the tofu, lemon juice, vinegar, garlic, miso paste and blend until creamy. Use immediately or store in the refrigerator for up to 3 days.

SWAP IT: This recipe makes a savory sour cream. If you want a neutral flavor—for baking, perhaps—omit the miso and garlic.

PER SERVING (¼ CUP): Calories: 76; Saturated Fat: 1g; Total Fat: 4g; Protein: 8g; Total Carbs: 3g; Fiber: 1g; Sodium: 34mg

CASHEW CREAM

PREP TIME: 30 minutes │ **MAKES:** 2 cups │ Gluten-free, Soy-free │ 5-ingredient, No-cook, Quick

The consummate plant-based condiment! When soaked and blended, cashews lend a rich, creamy texture to dishes without added dairy products or thickeners. I'm opting for a sweet version here because it's a great way to create quick and healthy treats, but see the tip below if you'd like to make it savory.

1 cup raw cashews

2 cups boiling water

2 tablespoons lemon juice

1 tablespoon pure
maple syrup

1 teaspoon pure
vanilla extract

1. In a small bowl, combine the cashews and boiling water and let sit for 30 minutes. Drain and rinse the cashews.

2. Transfer the cashews to a blender, add the lemon juice, maple syrup, and vanilla and purée, slowly adding ½ to ¾ cup water as needed until the mixture is thick and creamy.

3. Use immediately or store in the refrigerator for up to 5 days.

SWAP IT: For a smoky, savory cream sauce, skip the maple syrup and vanilla extract and add ½ teaspoon unseasoned rice vinegar, 2 teaspoons minced garlic, and 1 teaspoon smoked paprika.

PER SERVING (¼ CUP): Calories: 112; Saturated Fat: 1g; Total Fat: 8g; Protein: 3g; Total Carbs: 8g; Fiber: 1g; Sodium: 3mg

TEMPEH "BACON"

PREP TIME: 5 minutes | **COOK TIME:** 10 minutes | **MAKES:** 8 slices (8 ounces) | Gluten-free, Nut-free | Quick

This wholesome approach to bacon is proof that spices and seasonings rule. Smoky, salty, and slightly sweet are the name of the game for a cured-bacon-style flavor. Want a super-crispy vegan bacon with no frying? Pull out your air fryer and cook the tempeh at 330°F for 10 minutes, shaking the basket after 5 minutes. Raise the heat to 390°F and air-fry for 3 minutes more.

¼ cup Vegetable Broth
(page 180)
2 tablespoons pure
maple syrup
1 teaspoon soy sauce
½ teaspoon cayenne pepper
½ teaspoon smoked paprika
1 (8-ounce)
package tempeh

1. Preheat the oven to 375°F. Line a baking sheet with parchment paper.

2. In a small bowl, whisk together the broth, maple syrup, soy sauce, cayenne, and paprika to create a marinade.

3. Cut the tempeh lengthwise into 8 slices. Place them on the prepared baking sheet. Drizzle half the marinade over the tempeh and spread it evenly with a basting brush. Bake for 10 minutes, then flip the slices, brush the remaining marinade over the top, and bake for 8 minutes more.

4. Transfer the tempeh to a wire rack to cool. Serve immediately or store in the refrigerator for up to 5 days.

MAKE AHEAD: To make this bacon-style tempeh even more special, place the tempeh in a zip-top plastic bag. Combine the marinade ingredients in a measuring cup and pour the marinade into the bag. Seal the bag and turn it to coat the tempeh, then refrigerate overnight before baking. This added step creates a particularly tender tempeh bacon.

PER SERVING (2 SLICES): Calories: 138; Saturated Fat: 1g; Total Fat: 6g; Protein: 11g; Total Carbs: 12g; Fiber: 0g; Sodium: 79mg

PLANT PESTO

PREP TIME: 10 minutes | **MAKES:** 1½ cups | Gluten-free, Nut-free, Soy-free | No-cook, Quick

Basil and pine nuts are traditional in pesto. But we're not going for conventional here. We're going for a "pop," a "wow," and a nutrition boost. The coarse kale gives the verdant pesto an unexpected texture, and the pistachios lend a protein punch. If you're not big on garlic, cut back to 2 cloves.

2 cups tightly packed
  chopped stemmed
  kale leaves
½ cup shelled unsalted
  pistachios
3 garlic cloves,
  coarsely chopped
¼ cup nutritional yeast
2 teaspoons Spicy Umami
  Blend (page 196), or
  1 teaspoon kosher salt
¼ cup lemon juice
1 to 2 tablespoons
  extra-virgin olive oil
  (optional)

1. In a food processor, combine the kale, pistachios, and garlic and pulse until the nuts are ground into small bits.

2. While pulsing, add the nutritional yeast, umami blend, and lemon juice. With the motor running, slowly drizzle in the olive oil and process until a thick paste forms.

3. Use immediately or store in the refrigerator for up to 5 days.

INGREDIENT TIP: If you skip the oil here, you'll want to drizzle in a bit of water for texture and to make the pesto less thick.

PER SERVING (¼ CUP): Calories: 95; Saturated Fat: 1g; Total Fat: 5g; Protein: 6g; Total Carbs: 8g; Fiber: 3g; Sodium: 558mg

CAESAR DRESSING

PREP TIME: 10 minutes | **COOK TIME:** 20 minutes | **MAKES:** about 1½ cups | Gluten-free, Nut-free option | No-cook, Quick

Classic Caesar dressing, with its Worcestershire sauce, anchovies, and cheese, is not traditionally plant-based, but we can retain some of its essence with lots of umami. It is really perfect spooned over crisp romaine leaves, works great as a dip for vegetables and crackers, and makes a wonderful stand-in for mayonnaise.

¼ cup Tofu Sour Cream (page 181)

3 tablespoons Boozy Brown Mustard (page 188)

1 teaspoon rice vinegar

4 teaspoons minced garlic

¼ cup nutritional yeast

¼ cup chopped walnuts

2 tablespoons capers

¼ teaspoon freshly ground black pepper

1. In a blender or food processor, combine the sour cream, mustard, vinegar, and garlic and purée, stopping and scraping down the sides as needed, until smooth.

2. Add the nutritional yeast, walnuts, capers, and pepper and pulse a few times to incorporate.

3. Use immediately or store in an airtight container in the refrigerator for up to 1 week.

SWAP IT: I love any kind of brined veggie here as a substitute for the capers—try ¼ cup chopped pitted green or black olives.

ALLERGEN TIP: To make this nut-free, opt for hemp seeds instead of walnuts.

PER SERVING (¼ CUP): Calories: 70; Saturated Fat: 0g; Total Fat: 4g; Protein: 5g; Total Carbs: 4g; Fiber: 1g; Sodium: 86mg

"MEATY" MARINARA

PREP TIME: 5 minutes | **COOK TIME:** 35 minutes | **MAKES:** 4 cups | Gluten-free, Nut-free, Soy-free | One-pot

Consider this a pantry-friendly approach to a sauce everyone should have in their cooking routine. I make this staple weekly, and sure, it's great over pasta. But it's also terrific over baked potatoes or sautéed or steamed vegetables, and we use it as pizza sauce, too.

¼ teaspoon
  balsamic vinegar
4 to 6 teaspoons
  minced garlic
1 cup diced yellow or
  sweet onion
2 cups chopped shiitake
  mushrooms
1 teaspoon dried basil
1 teaspoon dried oregano
1 teaspoon dried parsley
1 teaspoon dried thyme
½ teaspoon red
  pepper flakes
1 teaspoon pure
  maple syrup
2 teaspoons Spicy Umami
  Blend (page 196)
¼ teaspoon freshly ground
  black pepper
1 (28-ounce) can crushed
  tomatoes
½ cup Vegetable Broth
  (page 180)

1. In a large saucepan, heat the vinegar over medium-high heat. Add the garlic, onion, and mushrooms and sauté until the onion softens, about 3 minutes. Add the basil, oregano, parsley, thyme, red pepper flakes, maple syrup, spice blend, black pepper, tomatoes, and broth, stir to combine, and bring to a boil.

2. Lower the heat to low, cover the pot with the lid ajar, and simmer for 30 minutes. Remove from heat.

3. Serve as desired or store in an airtight container in the refrigerator for up to 5 days.

INGREDIENT TIP: To make the sauce even "meatier," chop up the mushrooms in a food processor with ¼ cup walnuts, then add the mixture to the saucepan.

PER SERVING (1 CUP): Calories: 114; Saturated Fat: 0g; Total Fat: 3g; Protein: 5g; Total Carbs: 21g; Fiber: 5g; Sodium: 346mg

BOOZY BROWN MUSTARD

PREP TIME: 5 minutes, plus 2 days marinating | **MAKES:** about 1¼ cups | Gluten-free option, Nut-free, Soy-free | 5-ingredient, No-cook

Which came first: my love for beer or my love for coffee? It doesn't matter because both ingredients make this simple mustard stand out. We're a household of two, and this recipe can last us a month. If you have a larger family, you can easily double it.

½ cup brown mustard seeds
½ cup stout beer or
  cold-brewed coffee or
  espresso
¼ cup apple cider vinegar
1 teaspoon sea salt
2 tablespoons chopped
  pitted dates

1. In a pint jar, combine all the ingredients and ½ cup water. Cover, shake well, and set aside at room temperature for up to 2 days.

2. Transfer the mixture to a blender and purée until smooth but with a few flecks of mustard seed remaining.

3. Transfer the mustard to a clean airtight container and store in the refrigerator for up to 3 weeks.

SWAP IT: Substitute yellow mustard seeds, or use a combination of brown and yellow.

PER SERVING (1 TABLESPOON): Calories: 12; Saturated Fat: 0g; Total Fat: 0g; Protein: 0g; Total Carbs: 1g; Fiber: 0g; Sodium: 59mg

BBQ SAUCE

PREP TIME: 10 minutes | **COOK TIME:** 25 minutes | **MAKES:** 2 cups | Gluten-free, Nut-free, Soy-free option | One-pot, Quick

Here is another condiment that's great for burgers and sandwiches or brushed on vegetables while grilling. The smoky flavor brings out a meaty essence in all kinds of foods.

2 tablespoons Vegetable Broth (page 180)

½ cup chopped onion

2 garlic cloves, minced

1½ cups Smoky Ketchup (page 193)

¼ cup apple cider vinegar

2 teaspoons Spicy Umami Blend (page 196)

1 teaspoon chipotle chile powder

1. In a medium saucepan, heat the broth over medium-low heat. Add the onion and garlic and cook, stirring, for 5 minutes, or until softened.

2. Reduce the heat to low and add the ketchup, vinegar, Spicy Umami Blend, 1 tablespoon water, and the chipotle powder. Cover and simmer for 20 minutes.

3. Remove from the heat and let cool. Store in an airtight container in the refrigerator for up to 3 weeks.

SWAP IT: At this point in the book, you know JL loves chipotle chile powder. But there are a few other ways to bring out a smoky, umami essence when you don't have any chipotle powder on hand. Try smoked paprika, cayenne pepper, or a combination of the two.

PER SERVING (1 TABLESPOON): Calories: 57; Saturated Fat: 0g; Total Fat: 0g; Protein: 0g; Total Carbs: 15g; Fiber: 0g; Sodium: 67mg

BUFFALO SAUCE

PREP TIME: 10 minutes | **COOK TIME:** 20 minutes | **MAKES:** about 1½ cups | Gluten-free, Nut-free, Soy-free option | 5-ingredient, One-pot, Quick

Classic Buffalo sauce is pretty basic: butter, garlic, and hot sauce. I remain loyal to Frank's RedHot hot sauce, but use what you love. I like to add a little balsamic vinegar for a larger hit of acid. This sauce can be the base for Buffalo Cauliflower Pizza (page 132), but the most common use in our kitchen is as a marinade for tofu, tempeh, and seitan.

½ cup Plant Butter
   (page 179) **or other**
   vegan butter
2 garlic cloves, minced
1 cup hot sauce
1 tablespoon
   balsamic vinegar

1. In a small saucepan, combine the butter and garlic and cook over medium-high heat until the butter begins to bubble. Whisk in the hot sauce and vinegar and cook, whisking, until the mixture just begins to boil again.

2. Remove from the heat and use immediately, or let cool and store in an airtight container in the refrigerator for up to 1 week.

SMART SHOPPING: The first time I visited our local Asian Pacific Market, I was blown away by the long aisle filled exclusively with hot sauces! I encourage you to play around with different brands—they all vary by heat level—to find the one you love the most.

ALLERGEN TIP: To make this soy-free, use a soy-free vegan butter.

PER SERVING (2 TABLESPOONS): Calories: 72; Saturated Fat: 1g; Total Fat: 8g; Protein: 0g; Total Carbs: 1g; Fiber: 0g; Sodium: 184mg

RED CHILI PASTE

PREP TIME: 10 minutes | **COOK TIME:** 20 minutes | **MAKES:** 1¼ cups | Gluten-free, Nut-free, Soy-free | Quick

After buying many small plastic jars of spicy red sauce for our Asian meals, we just *had* to figure out a way to make it ourselves. Try playing with the heat level of your chile selection, which my husband I have done because we have varying reactions to heat. The compromise is using hotter peppers but removing their seeds.

12 ounces Anaheim (mild) or cayenne (hot) peppers

2 garlic cloves, coarsely chopped

1 small sweet onion, quartered

¼ cup Vegetable Broth (page 180)

2 teaspoons Spicy Umami Blend (page 196)

¼ teaspoon freshly ground black pepper

1. In a food processor, combine the peppers, garlic, and onion and pulse until finely chopped.

2. In a large saucepan, bring the broth to a boil over medium-heat. Add the pepper mixture and stir to combine. Lower the heat to medium-low and cook, stirring occasionally, for 15 minutes.

3. Add the umami blend and black pepper and cook for 5 minutes more.

4. Transfer the mixture back to the food processor and purée until smooth.

5. Transfer to an airtight container and store in the refrigerator for up to 10 days.

SWAP IT: The Spicy Umami Blend is excellent in this, but adding a little soy sauce or a pinch or two of kosher salt may be more to your liking.

PER SERVING (1 TABLESPOON): Calories: 13; Saturated Fat: 0g; Total Fat: 0g; Protein: 0g; Total Carbs: 3g; Fiber: 0g; Sodium: 9mg

SMOKY KETCHUP

PREP TIME: 10 minutes | **COOK TIME:** 20 minutes | **MAKES:** about 3 cups | Gluten-free, Nut-free, Soy-free option | 5-ingredient, No-cook, One-pot Quick

I've never met a potato that I didn't want to dip in ketchup, so I needed a recipe for this everyday staple, which is so easy to make at home and gives me total control of the ingredients. I keep it in a jar, but a squeeze bottle works great, too.

2 (6-ounce) cans tomato paste

⅓ cup red wine vinegar

2 teaspoons red miso paste

1½ teaspoons smoked paprika

¼ cup pure maple syrup or agave syrup

1. In a saucepan, whisk together all the ingredients and ⅔ cup water. Cook over low heat for 5 minutes, being careful not to let the mixture simmer. Remove from the heat. Depending on what you're using the ketchup for, you may want to add a little bit of water to make it less thick.

2. Transfer the mixture to a small 8-ounce jar or squeeze bottle and store in the refrigerator for up to 2 months.

SWAP IT: If you'd like to omit the maple syrup or agave, combine 2 or 3 pitted large dates and ¼ cup water in a blender and blend until smooth, then add the puréed dates to the saucepan with the rest of the ingredients.

ALLERGEN TIP: To make this soy-free, use chickpea miso paste.

PER SERVING (1 TABLESPOON): Calories: 11; Saturated Fat: 0g; Total Fat: 0g; Protein: 0g; Total Carbs: 3g; Fiber: 0g; Sodium: 13mg

CHEESY CHICKPEA SAUCE

PREP TIME: 10 minutes | **COOK TIME:** 10 to 15 minutes | **MAKES:** about 2½ cups | Gluten-free, Nut-free Soy-free option | Quick

A simple, pourable cheesy sauce is a great way to dress up steamed, roasted, or stir-fried vegetables. It's also lovely as an alternative spread for sandwiches and wraps, or as a topping for tacos and tostados. I will even stir this into marinara sauce or soups to make them creamy.

1 small sweet potato
1 (15-ounce) can chickpeas, drained and rinsed
¼ cup nutritional yeast
2 tablespoons miso paste
1 teaspoon ground turmeric
1 teaspoon Spicy Umami Blend (page 196)
1 tablespoon rice vinegar
Vegetable Broth (page 180), as needed

1. Fill a large saucepan with about 1 inch of water, insert a steamer basket, and bring to a boil over high heat. Lower the heat to medium-high and place the sweet potato in the steamer. Cover and steam for 12 to 15 minutes, until the potato is tender. Set the sweet potato aside until cool enough to handle, then remove and discard the skin.

2. In a blender or food processor, combine the flesh of the sweet potato, chickpeas, nutritional yeast, miso, turmeric, umami blend, and vinegar and purée until smooth. While blending, slowly add broth until the sauce is easy to pour but still thick.

3. Use immediately or transfer to an airtight container and store in the refrigerator for up to 5 days. Reheat the sauce in a saucepan with just a little water to thin it out before using.

ALLERGEN TIP: To make the sauce soy-free, use chickpea miso paste.

PER SERVING (½ CUP): Calories: 147; Saturated Fat: 0g; Total Fat: 2g; Protein: 8g; Total Carbs: 24g; Fiber: 6g; Sodium: 387mg

CARAMELIZED ONION JAM

PREP TIME: 10 minutes | **COOK TIME:** 25 minutes | **MAKES:** about 2 cups | Gluten-free, Nut-free, Soy-free | 5-ingredient

A dollop of this jam will take even something already tasty to the next level, like it does for the Apple Avocado Toast (page 56), Go-To Grits (page 61), and Vegetable Lentil Loaf (page 142). This condiment is even terrific schmeared over grilled or baked tofu or tempeh.

1 cup red wine
  vinegar, divided
3 large sweet onions, halved
  and thinly sliced
4 Medjool dates, pitted

1. In a skillet, heat ¼ cup of vinegar over medium heat. Add the onions and cook, stirring frequently, until soft and beginning to brown, about 15 minutes.

2. While the onions are cooking, in a food processor or blender, combine the dates and 2 tablespoons water and purée until a thick paste forms.

3. Add the date paste and remaining ¾ cup of vinegar to the onions and stir to combine well. Cover and cook, stirring occasionally, until the jam thickens, about 10 minutes.

4. Serve warm or at room temperature. Store in an airtight container in the refrigerator for up to 1 week.

SWAP IT: Play with the flavors by using different types of vinegar and dried fruit—try white wine vinegar and a dried apricot paste.

PER SERVING (¼ CUP): Calories: 79; Saturated Fat: 0g; Total Fat: 0g; Protein: 1g; Total Carbs: 18g; Fiber: 2g; Sodium: 12mg

SPICY UMAMI BLEND

PREP TIME: 5 minutes | **MAKES:** ¼ cup | Gluten-free, Nut-free, Soy-free | No-cook, Quick

True story: I wanted to call this the Um-bomb-i Blend. That didn't happen, but the name rings true: it's a flavor bomb! When I use this blend in place of salt, I tend to use double the quantity I'd use for salt. I've offered variations here with different levels of salt; as you use it, you'll discover the best balance for you.

¼ cup chopped dried
   mushrooms
1 tablespoon nutritional
   yeast flakes
1 tablespoon mustard seed
1 teaspoon cumin seed
1 teaspoon fennel seed
1 teaspoon red
   pepper flakes
1 teaspoon celery seed
2 teaspoons
   smoked paprika
1 teaspoon garlic powder

Combine all the ingredients in a blender or spice mill and grind to a coarse powder. Transfer to a jar, seal, and store in a cool, dark place for up to 3 months.

INGREDIENT TIP: My favorite dried mushrooms for this recipe are porcini, shiitake, and chanterelle. You will find them in the international aisle at your local grocer or at your local Asian market.

PER SERVING (½ TEASPOON): Calories: 3; Saturated Fat: 0g; Total Fat: 0g; Protein: 0g; Total Carbs: 0g; Fiber: 0g; Sodium: 15mg

LOW SALT
Add 1 teaspoon kosher salt.

GIMME SALT
Add 2 teaspoons
   kosher salt.

MISO CREAM SAUCE

PREP TIME: 10 minutes | **COOK TIME:** 10 minutes | **MAKES:** 3 cups | Gluten-free, Soy-free option | 5-ingredient, Quick

My cooking is heavily macrobiotic and Asian-influenced, as you've likely noted by now, and this cream sauce is the bridge that brings many of these recipes together. Use it over Buddha bowls, in savory porridge or oats, or as the final touch to any cooked vegetable. I like to drizzle it into mashed potatoes.

½ cup raw cashews

3 tablespoons white or yellow miso paste

2 cups unsweetened soy milk, divided

¾ cup Vegetable Broth (page 180)

1. In a high-speed blender, grind the cashews into a flour (be careful not to grind them into nut butter).

2. Transfer the cashew flour to a small bowl, add the miso and 1 cup of soy milk, and whisk to combine.

3. In a saucepan, bring the remaining 1 cup of soy milk and the broth to a boil over medium-high heat. Lower the heat to medium-low, add the cashew mixture, and bring to a simmer. Cook, whisking occasionally, until thick, 5 to 10 minutes.

4. Use immediately, or let cool and store in an airtight container in the refrigerator for up to 5 days.

ALLERGEN TIP: To make this soy-free, opt for nut, oat, or seed-based milk and use chickpea miso paste (brands include Miso Master, South River, and Thrive Market).

PER SERVING (½ CUP): Calories: 131; Saturated Fat: 1g; Total Fat: 7g; Protein: 6g; Total Carbs: 11g; Fiber: 1g; Sodium: 377mg

MEASUREMENT CONVERSIONS

Volume Equivalents (Liquid)

US STANDARD	US STANDARD (OUNCES)	METRIC (APPROXIMATE)
2 tablespoons	1 fl. oz.	30 mL
¼ cup	2 fl. oz.	60 mL
½ cup	4 fl. oz.	120 mL
1 cup	8 fl. oz.	240 mL
1½ cups	12 fl. oz.	355 mL
2 cups or 1 pint	16 fl. oz.	475 mL
4 cups or 1 quart	32 fl. oz.	1 L
1 gallon or 4 quarts	128 fl. oz.	4 L

Volume Equivalents (Dry)

US STANDARD	METRIC (APPROXIMATE)
⅛ teaspoon	0.5 mL
¼ teaspoon	1 mL
½ teaspoon	2 mL
¾ teaspoon	4 mL
1 teaspoon	5 mL
1 tablespoon	15 mL
¼ cup	59 mL
⅓ cup	79 mL
½ cup	118 mL
⅔ cup	156 mL
¾ cup	177 mL
1 cup	235 mL
2 cups or 1 pint	475 mL
3 cups	700 mL
4 cups or 1 quart	1 L

Oven Temperatures

FAHRENHEIT	CELSIUS (APPROXIMATE)
250°F	120°C
300°F	150°C
325°F	165°C
350°F	180°C
375°F	190°C
400°F	200°C
425°F	220°C
450°F	230°C

Weight Equivalents

US STANDARD	METRIC (APPROXIMATE)
½ ounce	15 g
1 ounce	30 g
2 ounces	60 g
4 ounces	115 g
8 ounces	225 g
12 ounces	340 g
16 ounces or 1 pound	455 g

REFERENCES

Appleby, P. N., G. K. Davey, and T. J. Key. 2002. "Hypertension and blood pressure among meat eaters, fish eaters, vegetarians and vegans in EPIC-Oxford." Public Health Nutrition 5(5):645–654.

Barnard, N. D., A. R. Scialli, G. Turner-McGrievy, A. J. Lanou, and J. Glass. 2005. "The effects of a low-fat, plant-based dietary intervention on body weight, metabolism, and insulin sensitivity." American Journal of Medicine 118:991–997.

Bradbury, K. E., F. L. Crowe, P. N. Appleby, J. A. Schmidt, R. C. Travis, and T. J. Key. 2014. "Serum concentrations of cholesterol, apolipoprotein A-I and apolipoprotein B in a total of 1694 meat-eaters, fish-eaters, vegetarians and vegans." European Journal of Clinical Nutrition 68(2):178–183.

Fraser, G. E. 2009. "Vegetarian diets: What do we know of their effects on common chronic diseases?" American Journal of Clinical Nutrition 89(5):1607S–1612S.

Manore, M. M. 2002. "Dietary recommendations and athletic menstrual dysfunction." Sports Medicine 32:887–901.

Phillips, S. M., S. A. Atkinson, M. A. Tarnopolsky, and J. D. MacDougall. 1993. "Gender differences in leucine kinetics and nitrogen balance in endurance athletes." Journal of Applied Physiology 75:2134–2141.

Poore J., and T. Nemecek. 2018. "Reducing food's environmental impacts through producers and consumers." Science 360:987–992.

Tantamango-Bartley Y. K. Jaceldo-Siegl, J. Fan, and G. Fraser. 2012. "Vegetarian diets and the incidence of cancer in a low-risk population." Cancer Epidemiol Biomarkers Prevention doi: 10.1158/1055-9965.EPI-12-1060.

Tonstad, S., K. Stewart, K. Oda, M. Batech, R. P. Herring, and G. E. Fraser. 2013. "Vegetarian diets and incidence of diabetes in the Adventist Health Study-2." Nutrition, Metabolism, and Cardiovascular Diseases 23(4):292–299.

Toth, M. J., and E. T. Poehlman. 1994. "Sympathetic nervous system activity and resting metabolic rate in vegetarians." Metabolism 43:621–625.

INDEX

ABOUT THE AUTHOR

JL Fields is a vegan chef, health coach, and chef consultant to food, health, and wellness brands. She is the founder and culinary director of the Colorado Springs Vegan Cooking Academy and a master vegan lifestyle coach and educator. JL is the author of several cookbooks: *Vegan Baking for Beginners*, *Fast & Easy Vegan Cookbook*, *Vegan Meal Prep*, *The Vegan Air Fryer*, and *Vegan Pressure Cooking*. She is the coauthor of *The Main Street Vegan Academy Cookbook* (with Victoria Moran) and *Vegan for Her* (with Virginia Messina). JL writes the monthly vegan dining review for the Colorado Springs *Gazette*. She produces vegan markets and the annual vegan restaurant week in Colorado Springs, where she lives with her husband, Dave, their rescued cat, Oliver, and their rescued dog, Harry.

Printed in the USA
CPSIA information can be obtained
at www.ICGtesting.com
JSHW070047220824
68427JS00006B/6

9 798886 083